Hedge Witchcraft

A Solitary Witch's Guide to Divination, Spellcraft, Celtic Paganism, Rituals, and Folk Magic

Your Free Gift
(only available for a limited time)

Thanks for getting this book! If you want to learn more about various spirituality topics, then join Mari Silva's community and get a free guided meditation MP3 for awakening your third eye. This guided meditation mp3 is designed to open and strengthen ones third eye so you can experience a higher state of consciousness. Simply visit the link below the image to get started.

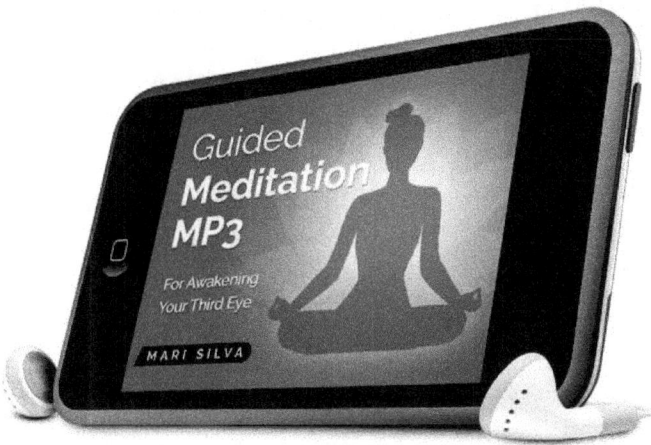

https://spiritualityspot.com/meditation

Table of Contents

INTRODUCTION 1

CHAPTER ONE: WHAT IS HEDGE WITCHCRAFT? 3

CHAPTER TWO: THE HEDGE MIND AND OTHER TOOLS
OF THE CRAFT 12

CHAPTER THREE: DEITIES YOU CAN WORK WITH 19

CHAPTER FOUR: HEDGE RIDING AND THE OTHER WORLD 28

CHAPTER FIVE: SPIRIT ALLIES AND HOW TO FIND THEM.........37

CHAPTER SIX: MAGICAL HERBS, PLANTS, AND TREES 49

CHAPTER SEVEN: HEDGE DIVINATION....................................57

CHAPTER EIGHT: KITCHEN MAGIC 67

CHAPTER NINE: SACRED SABBATS AND RITUALS........................76

CHAPTER TEN: YOUR HEDGE SPELL BOOK 86

CONCLUSION 101

HERE'S ANOTHER BOOK BY MARI SILVA THAT YOU
MIGHT LIKE..103

YOUR FREE GIFT (ONLY AVAILABLE FOR A LIMITED TIME) 104

REFERENCES 105

Introduction

Have you ever wondered what it would be like to perform hedge witchcraft? From traditional folklore, hedge witches use quick, easy-to-find ingredients found in most people's kitchens to create and cast spells for various purposes. Hedge witches, also known as cunning folk, have been around for centuries and perform their magical practices without anyone to supervise or teach them. Often called "the knowledge of the wise woman," hedge-witchcraft is based on folklore and encompasses magic traditions.

Hedge witchcraft can be used by anyone who has an interest in magic, whether they are a beginner or more experienced. Anyone who wants to increase their magical ability will find many uses for this powerful form of magic. However, this book is not open to anyone who desires to use hedge witchcraft dangerously or hurt others. You must be sure that you only use the craft for good, which means following written instructions and setting positive intentions. Why? Because anyone can use hedge-witchcraft tools to harm another person if they do not follow the rules and understand exactly what they are doing.

Traditional hedge witchcraft uses charms, incantations, and herbal remedies to accomplish goals. However, there are no specific rules of practice regarding hedge witchcraft. Many traditionalists practice alone or with a group of fellow practitioners. The purpose of this book is to provide a solid foundation for those looking for further personal development by practicing traditional hedge witchcraft. If you are already a practitioner, you'll get even more information about the craft from this book. Nothing in this book is intimidating or difficult to learn. You'll get all the tools you need to get started, including lists of required basic materials. With these lists and by following the simple directions, anyone can practice hedge witchcraft.

The mysticism behind the practice of hedge witchcraft is simple but effective. The use of common household herbs, such as sage and thyme, evokes the mystical effects of magic once commonly practiced in Europe. Although these methods seem quite primitive in today's world, many people are still practicing under these guidelines. Unlike other books on this topic, this one is written in simple English, making it easy to understand. The instructions are straightforward, in a step-by-step approach that takes you by the hand and walks you through what you need to do to achieve your goals with hedge witchcraft. The result is that you can practice what you learn in this book with the confidence of a seasoned hand. You will learn about the roots of the practice of hedge witchcraft, the concepts behind it, spells, and charms for different purposes, such as love, protection, healing, etc. Not only will you find out what ingredients you need to perform each spell or ritual here, but you'll also know what each one is for. If you're ready to begin your journey as a hedge witch, let's get into it.

Chapter One: What Is Hedge Witchcraft?

Practicing hedge witchcraft is like channeling information from nature, from the Earth itself. The practitioner of hedge witchcraft can attune themselves to natural cycles and energies we don't encounter in everyday society. The practitioner of hedge witchcraft becomes a part of their environment more subtly, giving their perception an empathic boost and the ability to be more connected with their surroundings.

The craft comprises aspects of green magic, kitchen magic, and folk magic, along with spirit work, animism, and Celtic paganism. So, without further ado, let's get into these topics, so you can gain a better understanding of what hedge witchcraft is.

Green Magic

As its name suggests, this magic works with plants, crystals, gems, and their energies. You can use them as a form of therapy for the spirit or magical intentions. The green witch always works with herbs and is very in touch with nature. The idea is that there is power in the color green since it is one of the most abundant colors of Mother Nature. It's useful for healing and abundance.

Green witches work with herbs.
https://unsplash.com/photos/kcvRHtAyuig?utm_source=unsplash&utm_medium=referr al&utm_content=creditShareLink

The green witch will follow a set of values aligned with nature and the Earth. Those who practice this form of magic are usually closely in touch with their energetic life force and celebrate regular rituals and rites. They work with divination, herbalism, and healing, believing that plants have specific energy, just as crystals do. For example, the moon, sun, and planets are all-powerful energy sources. Anyone who practices green magic believes that all these energies are active and that the more you can connect with them, the better you will feel.

Green witches believe in the power of flowers. They take the wonder of blooming flowers very seriously and work with them regularly to help them to find balance and peace. The green witch will often use the power of flowers during healing and also use them during magical ceremonies.

Green magic focuses on nature, the Earth, and all it offers. Followers believe in working with Mother Nature, celebrating her, helping her when she needs help, and working alongside her to achieve balance.

Kitchen Magic

Kitchen magic involves everything about the kitchen and cooking. It's a fusion of cuisine and witchcraft. The entire practice revolves around food and how you can combine different ingredients to produce magical effects. Every spice and herb used in cooking has a very real effect on our energies, and the kitchen witch knows how to combine and amplify them to help those who eat from her table.

To feel the power of kitchen magic, you must include all the things that please you and make you happy in your cooking. You should include complementary ingredients to what you cook, so they bring out the best in the meal. It's funny how some people don't value their kitchen as much as they should, let alone the process of feeding themselves or others. Making a meal from scratch with your own hands can be very magical, and it makes it even better to enjoy the works of your hands or enjoy the fact that everyone else is being fed thanks to your work, physically and spiritually. In other words, kitchen magic is a craft that encourages mindfulness, and mindfulness is a state that allows the power of magic to be even more pronounced.

The goal of this practice is to be able to create harmony in your own home. You should be able to connect with people who eat at your table and make them feel at home. To practice this form of magic, you need to be at home with your kitchen and the ingredients you've got, making sure you're always stocked for whatever magical needs you may have.

It is helpful to have an altar in the kitchen for this practice. You could consider the kitchen stove the same as the historical hearth, where every kitchen witch would prep her food. You want a portable altar; on it, you can put your candle, cauldron, a statue of your goddess, or whatever you want. It's also essential that the kitchen space be kept clean, not just physically but spiritually. It's easy to assume that all you need to do is wipe things down, and that's the end of that. In reality, you need to use sage to keep the place spiritually clean.

Suppose you're going to practice as a kitchen witch. In that case, it can be as simple as infusing every meal prep moment with magical intentions. For instance, you could intend that every ingredient you touch will generate love, healing, or abundance for those who enjoy the meal. You can also bring the other people around you in on the magic by having them mindfully set intentions for the meal you've prepared before everyone digs in to eat. Every spoonful of food could be used as a magical ritual to help you manifest your desires.

Folk Magic

This is the kind of magic of the common folk, and it's nothing like the ceremonial magic associated with those you think of as "elite." This is a very practical form of magic, and its intention is to deal with simple things like bringing more love and luck into your life, healing you, keeping bad energies away from you and your loved ones, helping you attain abundance, fertility, or finding what you've lost, as well as being able to recognize omens. The rituals performed in this kind of magic are simple and involve materials like wood, plants, twine, feathers, nails, animals, iron, eggshells, cowries, and so on.

It is important to note that folk magic is the type practiced by specific cultures and traditions. They will have specific rules for how you should interact with the world. Folk magic has many elements other kinds of magic borrow from, and, as a result, it can be confusing trying to differentiate it from other forms of magic. However, it all stems from the same ancient practices, which can be adapted to what you need them to be. Folk magic isn't connected to one specific religion, and there isn't a pantheon of specific gods that need to be worshiped. You don't need to adhere to a specific body of beliefs either. So, you could be a Buddhist or an Atheist and practice this form of magic and get phenomenal results.

Folk magic is all about sacred tradition. The term "sacred tradition" is one of the most common names given to traditional beliefs, customs, and practices that are important to people in a society. They're passed down from generation to generation, and people often look to them for guidance, wisdom, and comfort when such things are needed. This kind of magic looks at the world around us in tiny details and makes a safety net out of them.

You'll see small symbolic gestures have a huge impact on your life.

Spirit Work

It's a little hard to explain, but Spirit Work is a name we've given the practice of connecting with the spiritual energies around us. We work with specific aspects of these energies and entities. While that seems pretty abstract, it has real-world effects on people daily.

The idea is that you are connecting with the spiritual energies in your life. Everyone experiences these energies to one degree or another, but not everyone is focused on them. Spiritual energy is a part of everything and flows all around us. You know when you are in a good place, and you feel great? That's because there is spiritual energy all around you that is in alignment, causing things to go right. Spirit work lets you take advantage of this energy instead of waiting and hoping that things begin to go your way. You can harness the energy and channel it to whatever real-world results you want to accomplish.

Spirit work involves being in touch with spirits to perform magic. It means working with spiritual practitioners like witches and shamans, as they can traverse the realms between worlds that we cannot detect with our physical eyes. Wiccans also do spirit work by casting magic circles to contact spirits to enlist their help. As for witches, they don't need magic circles. Mediums are the ones who make spirit work available to the masses, helping regular people to contact the spirits of their loved ones who have passed on or other beings that do not exist in our world. This form of magic is something that came to be more popular as Spiritualism became more mainstream between 1840 and 1930.

Spirit work is also known as necromancy, which means conjuring the spirits of those who have passed on to learn about the future or how to change things for the better. These spirits can lend us their energies and knowledge to help the magical practitioner to perform their spells and rituals and get actual results from their work. For some practitioners, it's about ordering the spirits to do what they want. For others, it's about developing a relationship with these entities and respectfully enlisting their help in return for offerings.

Animism

The idea behind animism is that everything has its spirit. Whether you consider the thing to be living or nonliving doesn't matter. Everything has an essence with which you can interact. Animism is integral when it comes to spirituality. Every thing and every place has its own spirit, which is connected to the spirit of every other thing and people around them. It forms the core of various beliefs, practices, and forms of magic. Animism goes as far back as the Paleolithic era.

The word "animism" is from the Latin word anima, which means "life, spirit, or breath." it's the animating power that lies in all things and all beings. When it comes to animism, the idea is that you can draw on the spirits of the rocks, mountains, rivers, art, animals, plants, and more to perform your magical work. The idea of everything possessing a spirit is a very common one outside the Western world that they don't have a specific word that connotes the idea. It is taken for granted that all things are animated and that the life force within can be activated to do one's bidding.

Animism goes so far as to make clear that words and ideas are also imbued with their life force. Therefore, this school of thought holds that things like your name or the name of your hometown could have a very real effect on your life, for better or worse.

Celtic Paganism

The Celtic people of the Iron Age created their unique form of spirituality that mixed pagan and Christian elements. They were the first "pagans" to convert to Christianity due to the influence of missionaries from Iona in Scotland, but many of their stories and traditions had already disappeared.

Celtic paganism is polytheistic, meaning they worship and make sacrifices to more than one god. Many lesser gods may be connected to the more important gods. The Celtic people used many of the same religious symbols as people in other parts of the world did, but each group had its own variations.

Celtic is an adjective, not a noun, describing a group of people that lived in Europe before and during classical times. They spoke

Celtic languages and worshiped similar deities to those found in other areas with Celtic populations.

The Celts were spread out over a wide geographic area, and religious traditions varied greatly. However, there were some commonalities. Celtic religious practices included offerings to nature spirits and ancestors when asking for help to cure illness and provide prosperity. They used divination to learn the truth when needed and held festivals dedicated to the various gods.

What Is Hedge Witchcraft?

Hedge witchcraft is one of the more popular pagan paths. There are so many ideas about what it means to be a hedge witch, but the main characteristic of it is that it requires a lot of herbs and a strong connection with nature. You could also do magical work with your preferred goddesses and gods as a hedge witch. You can also act as a shaman and a healer or even affect the weather. That's the thing about being a hedge witch. It's a blend of all the other forms of crafts that we've covered.

Let's dig into the history of this form of witchcraft a bit because, for the most part, practitioners do just that to honor the past. Historically, witches were usually women and didn't live in the community of villagers. Instead, they lived on the fringes, usually on the hedgerows' other side. The hedge was a significant divider because, on one side, you would see the typical village life or civilization as it was back then, but on the other side, it was completely different. On the other side of the hedge lived the unknown, all the things the villagers considered wild.

The hedge witches acted as healers, helping those who needed help with some illness or injury. They were also rather cunning in their ways. As part of their job, they also took their time collecting essential plants and herbs from the deep forests and the hedges.

Hedge witchcraft was a solo craft that back then would be practiced alone. It was also not separate from daily life, in that even little acts like cleaning your home or making a nice pot of tea were considered a magical process, as you can imbue it with intentions for what you want to manifest. The hedge witch back then would learn her craft from other people in the family who had been practicing for a while and had honed their craft through practice. Sometimes you'll hear hedge witchcraft being called the green craft. At all times, you can expect to see a lot of influence from folk magic.

Like kitchen witchcraft, hedge witchcraft primarily revolves around the hearth and home, just as kitchen magic does. Your home is where you come from, representing your sense of stability. In your home, you feel grounded. Your home has a unique energy, affecting family and visitors who leave their own energetic imprint.

As hedge witchcraft revolves around the hearth and home, it is strongly rooted in the natural world. This means you must do a fair bit of herbal magic, including aromatherapy work. Often, hedge witchcraft involves using plants and herbs you've grown with your own hands. You'll likely have processed them on your own, drying what you need to and storing them in a way that works for you. You'll have looked into all your herbs, understood their energies, and learned how you could blend them all to make them work for you. The whole time, a true hedge witch also takes notes in a special grimoire so they can refer to the information later and not mix things up.

Advantages of Practicing Hedge Witchcraft

An advantage of practicing hedge witchcraft is that it doesn't require any formal training or initiation. A person can put on their first witch's hat and start practicing hedge witchcraft immediately if they want. People also say that being self-taught helps them identify with their abilities more than being taught by someone else, making them feel more comfortable experimenting with what they learn.

Another advantage of practicing hedge witchcraft is that it allows the practitioner to learn about witchcraft without having to shock their friends and family by telling them about their beliefs. It also allows them to learn about the craft without joining a coven or attending witchcraft classes.

Some say there are also disadvantages to practicing hedge witchcraft, particularly when you're going solo. They say they have mixed feelings about some of the practices they engage in because they aren't familiar with what other witches think is right or wrong and because whatever they have learned has come from books, magazines, websites, or other people's experiences. But the thing about this craft is you can't get it wrong as long as you know the basics and your intentions are clear and pure.

How can hedge witchcraft change your life for the better? It is great to help you to clear away distractions and to take control of your life. It's also good at allowing you to be more precise and precise in your abilities by learning to feel the energy around you and tweak it with your own.

Some people say that some of the best things they have accomplished in life have come after they began practicing hedge witchcraft, thanks largely to using the craft more effectively, developing better intuition about people and situations, and personal growth.

Are You a Hedge Witch?

1. Are you drawn to herbs?

2. Have you ever felt a connection to plants?

3. Do you get the sense that you can work magic with plants and herbs?

4. Do you feel a strong connection to nature?

5. Do you feel terrible if you haven't been out in nature for a while?

If you answered yes to at least three of these five questions, hedge witchcraft could be for you.

Chapter Two: The Hedge Mind and Other Tools of the Craft

The mind is the most important tool for practicing hedge witchcraft. In fact, the mind gives all other tools their power and effectiveness. As a result, mental discipline is crucial to the practice of hedge witchcraft. Mental discipline allows individuals to hone their psychic abilities, so they can more effectively connect with the natural world and receive positive outcomes in life while drawing down harmful influences from those around them.

What Is the Mind?

The mind is the consciousness of an individual. It connects to and interacts with the universe and everything in it, including other people, animals, nature, spirits, gods, goddesses, etc. With practice, individuals can enhance their connection to their minds and their minds' ability to recognize existing connections. In this way, they can develop a new understanding of themselves within the world around them and learn to control various situations and events that would otherwise be beyond their influence. To hedge witches, the mind is a powerful and useful tool that should be used to improve oneself and others.

How Can I Develop My Mind?

There are many practices an individual can perform to develop their mind. The most basic approach is to meditate or use some other type of focusing exercise where you become completely still and then focus on your thoughts, thus quieting the mind. Mindfulness and meditation are two very different concepts that can be practiced for many benefits.

The practice of mindfulness essentially allows an individual to become aware of the moment, what interactions are taking place, and also be aware of their thoughts and emotions. The practice of mindfulness helps you learn to recognize your physical and emotional states by becoming more connected to them. Practicing mindfulness could also help you control your emotions, which can be a powerful advantage when healing or restoring others.

Meditation is the practice of quieting one's thoughts and focusing on one thing, usually a crystal or candle flame. Meditation relaxes the mind and allows individuals to focus on the work that they are trying to do. Meditation can also help individuals to strengthen their psychic abilities by increasing their mental clarity. Connecting when confusing or chaotic thoughts aren't bombarding your mind is easier.

It is said that the human mind has two complementary parts. One part of the brain is used for logic and analysis, which helps you process information to make accurate decisions. The other part of the brain deals with feelings, memories, instincts, and intuition. You can use a greater portion of either or both parts by training your mind, depending on your goal. Turning your thoughts inward and connecting with the feeling part of your mind can enhance your psychic abilities and relationships with others.

Being mindful of your thoughts and emotions and connecting to feel-good emotions can help you overcome negative feelings from past experiences. This can be beneficial because past negative experiences are often based on feelings of loneliness, fear, or insecurity and can trigger the same feelings in you again. You need to be in a positive state of mind if you achieve your goals through hedge witchcraft. A positive mindset allows you to become more connected to life. In turn, this can help you become aware of opportunities often overlooked by others, which is essential when working with hedge witchcraft.

How to Get into the Right Mindset

1. **Meditate:** Just focus on your breathing and nothing else for about five to ten minutes each day. When your mind wanders (and it will), just be glad you noticed and bring your attention back to your breath. Do this as many times as you get distracted. You'll get better at this the more you practice, and soon it will be very easy to get into a state of Zen without needing much time or effort.

2. **Spend Time in Nature:** Take time to enjoy nature daily, even if it's just for five minutes. Enjoy the aromas, the feel of the air against your skin, listen to the sounds, and look at the plants and trees (or, in my case, listen to the birds). Each day you'll find you need less time in nature. And when you spend time in nature, ensure you have a positive attitude toward what you see. When your mind is focused on appreciation and beauty, your attitude will follow suit. You should also try walking on the ground barefoot, and it will center you.

3. **Enjoy the Positive Aspects of Your Life:** Enjoy the things that make you happy. Whether it's getting to sleep in, a meditative bath, a good workout, or just reading a good book – take time to enjoy and appreciate these things. Know that they can always be there; you're lucky to have them.

4. **Take Time for Yourself:** Take at least one day each week when you do not have to worry about your job, finances, bills, or any other stress. Give yourself the freedom to spend these hours sleeping in, going for a stroll in nature, or simply enjoying a cup of coffee and reading a book.

5. **Follow Your Passions:** Pursue activities you love and feel good while doing them. Find a hobby that you can do for a lifetime. You'll find you'll enjoy it more, and doing it will bring you joy – in the same way that anything else that brings you joy does.

Tools Needed in Hedge Witchcraft

You don't need to break the bank to get these tools. When you know the purpose of each one, you can work with regular materials around your home. For instance, you could use a cooking pot dedicated to your magic instead of a cauldron. If you want to buy tools specifically crafted for the craft but don't want to spend too much, consider checking Craigslist or eBay.

The Cauldron: A large pot (often round) used to prepare and cook food. This is the main tool that you will use to start witching. It must be made from copper and have a lid that fits well on top. An old saucepan, cast-iron pan, or baking dish can also work. Every witch owns one; it's a cliché, sure. But if you find yourself in a situation where your cauldron is ruined or out of use, and you don't have the funds to buy a new one, then consider renting one from a local theatrical store.

The Wand: A long, thin stick or branch used to direct energy. In many traditions, it is made from a tree branch. The wand must be made of wood and cannot be plastic or metal. In some aspects of magic, the wand also represents a phallic symbol, so if this makes you uncomfortable, then you can use something like a dowsing rod instead. It's not always used in witchcraft, but it is useful when you need to call upon the element of air, which is one of the major elements in most traditions.

The Mortar and Pestle: Used to crush and mix ingredients together. The mortar is just a bowl, and the pestle is the stick you rub inside it to crush ingredients. You need these two together to successfully handcraft your spells. Be sure to get one that fits well in your hand and is made of wood with a long handle.

Use a mortar and pestle to crush your materials.

The Athame: This tool is like a wand, but instead of directing energy, it cuts energy. It is used for cutting up herbs and candles. The athame is usually double-edged and made of metal so that it can effectively cut what you are working with. Also called a black-handled knife or a white-handled knife, depending on the tradition you are part of. This is also used for drawing symbols or words in the air. It can also be used for carving symbols into candles or working with a candle.

The Athame Sheath: This is a cover that you will use to keep your athame safe while not using it. You can make one yourself or buy one at many places, including online stores.

The Grimoire: A book of spells and rituals. It's a book of magic. This spiritual tool you'll use to write out and record your spells. You can and should have your own, but you can find published grimoires in bookstores, or sometimes you may find one at a library. These books also come in different styles and sizes. Be sure to get one that you can use comfortably and with room for your spell-writing needs. There are many on the market, but these can be expensive. An alternative is to look online for free spells, test those spells out, and then write them in your own grimoire. It's also known as the Book of Shadows.

The Bell: Is often used to clear energy in the area you are working in. You can also use it to call upon the elements of nature. The bell should be a small one that is not too loud but enough to catch your attention when it rings. A small bell or chime can also call on spirits or mark the end of a spell's spoken words.

Crystals and Stones: These are considered "energetic tools" that act as a mirror for the energy of an object. These can be used in several ways depending on what belief system you are part of. They can be used to create spells, call spirits, and communicate with them (through your own voice or a recording). Many witches also keep stones in their bags or pockets to ground themselves. Some stones are believed to hold magical powers and are used for protection. You can get these from various sources, but you must be careful where you get them; you need to be sure they are authentic. Some of the most common crystals used in witchcraft are quartz, amethyst, jasper, and citrine.

The Bellows: This tool is used for blowing out candles and sending energy into objects such as candles, incense, and crystals. You can also use it for blowing on a person to help them relax and sleep.

The Broom: Used to cleanse negative energy from an area, it is yet another common witch cliché. You can use a "real" broom, but it is unnecessary. You can also use a feather duster or a feather if you do not have access to any other tools. The broom is also used in some spells where a need arises to "sweep" something away (pushing energy downward instead of upward). It can also be used for cleaning the floor and walls during a spell. Many witches also use brooms to clear the air in an area during rituals or spell casting.

The Knife: Used to cut or slice herbs; one of these would also be useful while cooking at home. You could use scissors instead.

Divination Tools: These are used for readings and messages from spirits. You can also use them to find out information about a spell you want to make or the magical impact it will have on you, a person, or an object. Many traditions use tarot cards in various ways and can be used in conjunction with other tools. Runes are also used in some traditions, including witchcraft.

The Tarot Deck or Card Set: If you use a tarot deck or other divination tool, you will need to have a tool to shuffle the cards. Several decks exist, and the one that you choose should reflect the type of magical beliefs that you have. Most decks also come with a few spreads, such as "readings" and "expert readings," to help you to create your own spells and rituals. These are separate from the cards and do not need to cast spells. The images on cards can also have different meanings depending on which deck you use. You also get a book to help you interpret all of these meanings, which is almost always a great idea.

The Velvet Bag: This bag can hold small objects such as herbs that you may need during a spell, and it can also be used to hold your other tools during spell casting.

Sigils: Sigils are a visual picture to represent the magic that you want to do. They can be used to cast spells, draw power from objects, and create a spiritual connection. You can create your own or buy them, and there are also kits you can use to help you create your sigil. In many traditions, these symbols are carved into candles or other objects representing energy.

Small Jars and Containers: Used for holding herbs, spices, and other items. Symbols and sigils painted or drawn on the container can also help you to cast spells and call upon spirits.

Chapter Three: Deities You Can Work With

Hedge witchcraft has a deep connection to Celtic paganism. So, we'll talk about the important deities that the Celts honor. You don't have to work with all of these deities, and it's up to you to figure out who resonates with you the most and then work with them instead. When you have an energetic or spiritual bond with a deity, you can draw on that connection to imbue your rituals with power.

Brigid

Brigid is known as "the Exalted One." She rules over motherhood and fertility. If you're a poet, an inventor, into some sort of craft, or you're a very passionate person, you have her to thank for that. Pagans believe there are three parts to this goddess, just as is the case with some other deities, but the difference is that each part is named the same.

For some, there are a lot of parallels between Brigid the goddess and the Christian Saint Brigid of Kildare. She is believed to simply be the Catholic Church's attempt to syncretize the land's spirituality with their religion. Her symbol is a cross with three arms, sometimes four. This cross is made of rushes, and it is believed that if you want to keep yourself safe and protected, all you have to do is put it over your window or door at home, and she'll protect you.

This goddess influences life and springtime, when everything thrives and comes to life. She is in charge of the smithery and the one to turn to when you work with the healing arts. She is celebrated on Imbolc, which happens each year on the first of February, being the middle of winter. If you go to Ireland, you'll find that the people have dedicated most of the waterways and wells to this deity. Brigid is part of the Tuatha Dé Danann.

Originally, her name was Brid, until it was anglicized into the current form and the other names Bride, Brig, and Brigit. The goddess's name inspired the name Bridget, demonstrating her link to fire and the sun. It's also possibly connected to other Indo-European goddesses in charge of the dawn. She wears a sunbeam cloak, demonstrating her fire and passion, but she's also in charge of water and serenity. She can show up either as a mother figure or a lovely maiden. Her hair is reminiscent of fire itself, and she rules the dawn.

Brigid knows all there is to know about high architecture and inspires people in that field and other craftsmen. She is wise and a healer, both attributes she inherited from Dagda, her father, who reigned supreme in matters of mysticism and magic. She also knows what your true needs are at every moment. There is a well dedicated to her in Kildare, and its waters are used for healing and blessing. There's also another well dedicated to her in County Clare.

Brigid was the daughter of one of the chiefs of the Tuatha Dé Danann named Dagda, and thanks to him, she had many sisters and brothers, including Midir and Aengus. Danu, the river goddess, was her mother. Brigid had a son with Bres, her husband, named Ruadan. Some other lore holds that she was married to Tuireann instead and had three sons named Irchaba, Iuchar, and Brian. Her sons were responsible for killing Lugh's father, Cian. It is known that many strangers come to Brigid to ask her to heal, bless, and inspire them. She favors those who have good intentions and those who are cunning.

Worshiping Brigid

You can honor her on February 1. This is the start of the New Year in Ireland, and on this day, you can take coins and food offerings to any waterway close by to honor her. As you make your offerings, you can also ask her to protect, heal, guide, and inspire you. You can ask her to bless your family and children, or even your pets if you've got any. You may offer her water, fire, metals, and prayer. You could get ribbons and tie them to a tree in her honor. She also likes coins, ale, cakes, poetry, and eggs. Do you have a basket constructed from rushes? Bring that to her, and you will have her heart.

Cernunnos

This is the god in charge of the wild. He ruled over the beasts of the land and is often depicted as having a horn, with animals all around him. He is adept at brokering peace between enemies. There are several other horned gods he shares a link with, as well as the Green Man, Herne the Hunter, Silvanus, and Pan. There's proof that it was mostly the people of the land of Gaul who worshiped this horned god, though. You can refer to him as the horned one.

This god has a way of bringing peace between nature and humans, and he's the one who can tame animals to the point where predator and prey can find peace with each other. Sadly, his actual myth remains a mystery. His name, though, is a Gaelic word that means "horned one," and lately, it's become the name to use when referring to the other horned gods the Celts used to worship, whose names have now been forgotten. To neopagans, he is the "God of Wild Places" or the "Lord of the Wilds," both titles being very recent developments.

A man with a beard and antlers, either wearing or carrying a torc made of metal, is believed that his physical attributes are put together based on other deities from Rome and Greece who looked similar. He was basically a merger of several gods. He would bless his followers not only with animals but with vegetables and fruit. He's often depicted with snakes, aurochs, wolves, and an elk, all residing side by side because he can easily quash enmity between natural foes. This makes him the god to seek protection and provision from.

It is believed that Cernunnos has a connection to Conach Cernach, at least etymologically speaking. Conach Cernach is from the Ulster cycle. Cernunnos may also share some links to Shakespeare's Herne the Hunter, who killed himself rather than be perceived dishonorable. After his death, his spirit would haunt the wild, bringing terror to all the creatures it came upon.

Worshiping Cernunnos

As he has a torc, you can get one yourself that's dedicated to him; it's basically a necklace made of metal. He is typically honored on Beltane, which is on May 1, or November 1 if you're in the Southern Hemisphere. You can offer him sacred plants like grains, juniper, ivy, oak, and mistletoe. You can also bring him antler sheds, milk, soil, water, and wine. You can drum for him or perform sexual acts in his honor.

Cailleach

Cailleach is "the Veiled One." This goddess is in charge of winter and the winds and is often depicted as an old woman wearing a veil, sometimes having only one eye. Her skin is a shade of blue sometimes, though, at other times, it's incredibly pale. She has red teeth, and her dress is covered in skulls. She has both creative and destructive aspects, and she is the patron deity of wolves. Sometimes she is considered benevolent, and sometimes she's not to be messed around with because she's fearsome. While Brigid rules the summer, Cailleach is the goddess of winter. She had several marriages, but the most popular partner she ever had was Bodach, a trickster god with whom she had a lot of offspring.

The Queen of Winter determines how bad and long the winter gets. She was honored in the Isle of Man, Ireland, and Scotland, which are also her dwelling places. Cailleach translates to "hag" or "old woman" in Irish Gaelic and Scottish. She is also known as Birog, the fairy woman, Milucra, Bui (married to Lugh), Digde, Digdi, and Burach. The many names make some believe that she is a combination of several deities with similar traits.

The Veiled One can ride the storm, and she is so powerful that she can move over mountains in a single leap. She also has shape-shifting abilities. She has a hammer which she uses to create the new and destroy the old, and according to lore, she has power over thunder and storms. Sometimes she would wield her power over wells, making them overflow and destroy the land. You can't consider her a good or bad deity because, depending on the tale, she can be benevolent or malevolent. While she can be destructive, she has an unparalleled love for all animals, especially when the winter gets intense. She takes care of them.

This goddess is young, old, ageless, and immortal. When spring comes, she takes a draught that makes her young again. The Manx holds that she spends half the year as an old crone and the other half as a young maiden. So, she's known as Cailleach in the latter part of the year. According to the Irish, she had seven distinct periods when she was youthful, and after that, she remained old indefinitely.

Worshiping Cailleach

Cailleach doesn't need your worship, but if you want to honor her, you can simply spend time around mountains, caves, hills, rock formations, and other land formations. You can also spend time around natural bodies of water like whirlpools, rivers, and natural wells.

Cerridwen

She is the goddess of transformation, and she is also the ruler of knowledge and inspiration. Her name means "white crafty one" or "white sow." She is also known as the Grain Goddess, Nature Goddess, White Lady of Inspiration and Death, and the Dark Moon Goddess. She oversees magic, regeneration, death, and fertility. She rules the underworld, and her cauldron has the powers of rebirth, knowledge, and inspiration. She shows up in the lore surrounding Bran the Blessed, leaving her place in Ireland to dwell in the Land of the Mighty. She put on the disguise of Kymideu Kymeinvoll, a giantess, and she showed up with Llassar, her husband.

They both came out of a lake, which is essentially thought of as the underworld. The people feared the power they wielded, so they banished them. Bran offered the two of them safe harbor. All he wanted in return was Ceriddwen's cauldron, which could reanimate dead warriors whose bodies were put into it. Bran would eventually give Matholuch this cauldron during his marriage to Branwen, his sister. Cerridwen's cauldron combines the three known kinds of cauldrons: Transformation, Rebirth, and

Inspiration.

Cerridwen is responsible for bringing life into the world and always cooking up something in her cauldron. She is the spiritual representation of the wheel of life, which includes birth, death, and rebirth cycles. She's the one to call on when you would like some growth in terms of your spirituality or some good luck in your physical life. She can also bring you abundance and nurture you. Small wonder then that her color is green, the very color of nature, which is abundant and gives freely to one and all.

Worshiping Cerridwen

To honor this goddess, you can offer her pork, acorns, vervain, grains, and other cereals. You should also work with your cauldron in her honor. You can find ways to incorporate the symbols that represent her, such as the dark moon, which represents her dark connection to magic, the moon in its various phases, and the white sow.

Herne

Also known as Herne the Hunter, he is considered a specter than a deity. He was responsible for putting man and animals through torment, and before you saw this antlered being, you would hear chains rattling and voices moaning. Some consider him to have been one of the aspects of Cernunnos. He would haunt the Berkshire woods often and always showed up on a mighty steed. Herne had a tree in Windsor Forest, his favorite haunt, known as Herne's Oak.

When it comes to his powers, he can make the natural world decay. All he needs to do is touch a finger to a tree, which would shrivel and die. He could also cause cattle to give blood rather than milk. According to folklore, he had a horn and would often travel in the company of hounds. When he shows up, it's believed something terrible is about to happen. He's a very mysterious deity, mostly because he rarely interacts with anyone when he encounters people. What is sure, though, is that his energy is cruel, and it could be because of how he died — by taking his own life.

Some believe that Herne was related to the Norse god of the dead, Odin. Odin is synonymous with Wotan and was in charge of the Wild Hunt, a quest to rally souls that had passed on for his army of the dead. Herne became popular during the Victorian era, just like the Baphomet, a horned god, and demon. He is a common god for English neopagan movements.

Worshiping Herne

You can offer this god some whiskey, cider, and mead. You can also offer him some meat. If you hunted the meat yourself, it's even better. Try burning some incense for him, especially the kind with dried autumn leaves. He considers this smoke sacred, and you can use it to send your requests to him so that he can give you a speedy response.

Lugh

He's the god of justice. He's the one who ensures oaths are kept and is also in charge of nobility. This god is considered a trickster god with the capacity to save those in trouble. He is well known for his successful war tactics and his excellent craftsmanship. Not only is he considered a warrior king, but he's also a hero to the Irish. His wife had a lover named Cermait, whose three sons would kill him by driving a spear through his foot and then drowning him. This was in response to his killing of Cermait. Lugh had the legendary Spear of Assal, and it was near impossible for anyone to escape being hurt by that weapon when he wielded it against them.

Sometimes, Lugh is also known as Lug, and it is hypothesized that the name comes from Proto-Indo-European roots, from the word *lewgh,* which means "to bind by oath." This makes sense because Lugh was particular about contracts being honored to the letter. Some say the name means "light," but no one is completely sure. He made sure that justice was served, and he would execute judgment with speed and with no room for reconsideration. Yet, he also had a penchant for being a trickster. This meant he had no problem stealing, lying, and cheating to ensure he had the upper hand over his enemies.

Worshiping Lugh

Lugh is worshiped on Lughnasa, also known as Lughnasadh. This Irish festival is held on August 1, celebrated in the Isle of Man, Ireland, and Scotland. It's a significant day because it was when Lugh triumphed over the Tir na nOg spirits. To mark this occasion, he granted an early harvest of fruits and honored his Tailtiu, his foster mother, by hosting some games. This day is also known in Christianity as Mountain Sunday or Garland Sunday. You can offer him bread, grains, corn, and anything else that represents the idea of harvest.

Morrigan

This Irish goddess is in charge of destiny, battle, and death. She has three aspects to her, all sisters, and can also show up as just one being. She rules fate and is in charge of the gift of prophecy. No matter who approached her, whether a deity or a hero, she would do them favors and offer them prophecy. You can see her as a raven flying around a battlefield, waiting for the carrion she can eat and take away. She also had the power of shapeshifting; whenever she showed up, it was considered a terrible omen because someone was sure to die. Sometimes, you'll hear her or them referred to as "The Morrigan." She is also known as the Great Queen or the Phantom Queen.

This prophetess can show up not just like a raven but as an old crone, a young, beautiful maiden, and a warrior queen with fierceness in her gaze. Since she is connected to fate and prophecy, it's not unusual to learn that she's connected to the death of mighty individuals. She showed up as a raven on Ulster as he died. She also shows up as a washerwoman with something strange and otherworldly about her. In this case, you'll find her bloody and washing clothes that belonged to those who have passed on in battle.

This is a goddess with three aspects. Depending on who you ask, their individual names are Badb, Macha, and Nemain. Other times, Nemain is known as Dannan, Danu, Anand, or Anu. It is Badb that shows up as a raven during battle. Note that each aspect or sister can act on her own. Nemain and Badb have a thing for giving deathly screeches so terrifying that at least 100 men who hear them at night die because they're frightened, and with good reason. That shriek means terrible things to come, and their deaths could well be considered merciful compared to the onslaught they would have otherwise witnessed.

Worshiping the Morrigan

It's a good idea to leave her offerings regularly, as the more you do, the more power you generate for your rituals. Craft a separate altar for her if you can. If not, create a space just for her on your altar. You can offer her stormwater, red wine, red foods, honey, mead, milk, a boline knife, feathers from a crow, poetry, art, and foods native to Ireland.

You can offer red wine to Morrigan.
https://pixabay.com/images/id-541922/

Chapter Four: Hedge Riding and the Other World

Hedge riding is also known as hedge jumping or hedge flying. This skill is necessary if you're going to be a hedge witch, but what is it exactly? The word "hedge" can take on various connotations in hedge witchcraft, and one of them is the boundary that separates this physical world from the spiritual one, otherwise known as the Otherworld. The hedge acts to keep humans and spirits apart from each other. When you hear of a hedge witch "riding the hedge" or "flying the hedge," what's going on is the witch is crossing over, going through the veil from the physical world to the spirit world.

So, hedge riding is taking a spiritual trip into the realm of spirit, where the collective unconscious lies. This act is shamanic, reminiscent of traveling to the astral realm. In other words, it's pretty much the same thing as astral projection. Usually, it's something you do on your own as a hedge witch, although some witches like to work together to have more insight and value to share from their journeys. You can perform rituals and spells as a group in the Otherworld if that's what you'd like to do. The good thing about riding the hedge with others is that you can have someone else's perspective on things, which could help you consider matters you may not have thought about.

Hedge Riding, Shamanic Travels, and Astral Projection

The difference between hedge riding and shamanic travels is that the witch isn't getting into psychopomp affairs. She doesn't help souls to move on to their next journey. Instead, she travels to gain insight and knowledge, heal, and practice divination, meditation, and her craft. Hedge riding is also different from shamanic travels because the hedge witch doesn't seek to control her journey. Instead, she goes along with the ride and doesn't attempt to control what happens next. She is, however, in charge of her actions. While astral projection often happens in our own level of existence (as well as several others), hedge riding is meant to get you to the Otherworld itself.

To be clear, hedge riding isn't a function of visualization or imagination. It is the actual process of leaving the physical world. You have to keep in mind that you don't control the journey you experience. If you aren't careful and respectful of the process, you may encounter dangerous forces that could cause you harm.

Before you can hedge ride, you must enter a state of altered consciousness. There are many ways to do this, such as chanting, meditation, dancing, drumming, and even taking certain psychedelic medicines. It's much better not to use drugs as a pathway to altered consciousness because you may encounter more danger as you cannot control yourself. However, in the past, the hedge witch used magical ointments to help her transition from the physical world to the Otherworld by inducing a state of altered consciousness.

The Otherworld and Hedge Riding

There are three distinct aspects to the Otherworld; the Upper, Middle, and Lower realms. Each of these worlds has nine levels. One form of this world is the Yggdrasil, the World Tree of Norse mythology. Now let's talk about the Havamal, a collection of verses in the 13th century Poetic Edda. The 156th verse has two translations and talks about the process of flying the hedge. You can use either translation of this verse to make the hedge rider reveal who they truly are, head back to their home, or keep their spirit apart from their body. The bottom line is that it's clear from these verses that hedge riding is an actual practice and that often, travelers take on a form different from their physical one. The better you get at hedge riding, the more you'll be able to shape-shift into different creatures to stay safe. Usually, the hedge rider will travel with animal guides to keep themselves safe and guide them along their journey through worlds unknown.

This is a dangerous practice only if you allow yourself to be overwhelmed with fear, an energy that will draw negative entities to you. You must recognize that you have every right to travel to the Otherworld and that you're a sovereign being with autonomy over yourself. If you don't, trickster spirits and malevolent entities could take advantage of you. This is why taking precautions before you fly the hedge is important. You shouldn't be afraid because there's a lot of good to be experienced from the Otherworld that makes the process worth it for you as a hedge witch. Let's look at some rituals you can perform before crossing to Otherworld.

Cleansing Ritual

It is good practice to cleanse yourself and your space often, especially when you intend to work with spirits or cross over the hedge. Cleansing also ensures that they don't attach themselves to you or your space when you've finished working with the spirits. If you don't, you may notice that the energy in your home feels wrong and is even kind of heavy. Also, you may have a difficult time flying the hedge. So, you must begin cleansing to raise the vibrations of your space and your being. You can do routine cleanses but note that sometimes you need to go deeper because there are places where energy remains trapped, for example, in a closet that is often shut or a room you hardly go into. So now and then, get deep into cleansing.

You'll Need:

- 4 quartz crystals

- 3 amethyst crystals

- 1 malachite crystal

- 1 small white candle

- A picture or carving of a coyote (other scavenger animals like a vulture or raccoon will do as well)
- A bundle of sage
- 5 sage leaves (fresh or dried)
- 3 sprigs of rosemary (fresh or dried)
- Salt
- A broom
- Saltwater in a bowl
- Lighter or matches

Steps:

1. Clean your home from top to bottom, ensuring you don't neglect any spot. This means moving your furniture to get underneath it, opening closets and rooms to let them get air and light, removing all cobwebs, and so on. The idea is to stimulate the flow of energy. If you can't find the time or your home is properly cleaned and organized already, focus on removing dust from the floor.

2. After cleaning, move around your home from room to room and clap your hands. If there's somewhere you don't often go, clap there. Also, clap behind doors, beneath the couch and other furniture, and in corners of the rooms. This will awaken the energy there.

3. Next, set up your altar in a central location in your home, like the kitchen or your living room. Make sure it's not on the floor and has enough space to put all the items you'll be working with on it. Also, make sure it's in a space that will let you cast a circle of salt around it.

4. The image or carving of the coyote should be placed centrally onto your altar and a candle placed above or behind it.

5. Put the quartz crystals at each corner, ensuring they face outward.

6. Put the malachite to the south of the carving.

7. Place the amethyst in the other cardinal directions.

8. Put your sage leaves next to your quartz crystals.

9. Put one sprig of rosemary on the left and the other on the right (East and West).

10. Get your salt and create a circle all around the altar.

11. Now, it's time for you to invoke the spirit you seek to talk to. Say a short prayer to it, asking for its help with the cleansing ritual.

12. Next, light the candle, then proclaim that the candle's energy now purifies your home.

13. Now it's time to spread salt all over your floors. If they're carpeted, please use baking soda instead. You should make sure the salt gets everywhere.

14. When you've finished salting your floor, you should begin vacuuming or sweeping, moving from the Northwest direction to the Southeast while chanting that your home is now being swept clean of negative energy and that only love and joy fill it.

15. You'll have a heap of salt when you've finished. Flush it down the toilet, envisioning the negative energy going down the drain. If it's too much to flush, throw it in the garbage outside the home.

16. Take your other sage leaf and rosemary sprig and put it in your salt water. Use the rosemary sprig to sprinkle the water around your space in a counterclockwise motion. As you do this, say a short prayer affirming that you cleanse your home with water and earth and that only love and joy fill your home.

17. Light the sage and use the smoke to cleanse your space, working counterclockwise as you say a short prayer affirming you cleanse your home with air and fire, and only love and joy fill your home.

18. Meditate for about five minutes before your altar, noting the light feeling in your space when you've finished. Let the candle burn down, and thank your spirit for its assistance. When you've finished, take a bath to rid yourself of any negativity.

Protection Ritual

Protection is a matter of mindset. You need to realize nothing can harm you without your permission, and you grant permission to be harmed by being afraid or expecting to be hurt. You must remain unfazed by whatever you encounter as you hedge ride. However, a simple practice you can do is imagine yourself being surrounded by golden light. Picture this light as an eggshell around you, keeping everything and anyone who means you harm away from you. You can make it as big or bright as you want. As you're in the Otherworld, it will show up around you and effectively keep you safe.

Grounding Ritual

1. Plant your feet firmly on the ground.
2. Imagine your feet growing roots into the core of the Earth.
3. Feel yourself taking in the Earth's energy through the soles of your feet from the earth up and through the rest of your body.
4. Breathe deeply for a minute or more as you feel the energy flowing through you. You will notice that you feel calmer and more present. When you do, you'll know you've done it right.

How to Hedge Ride

To let your spirit separate from your body, you have to alter your state of consciousness. You can do this naturally or through induction. Please avoid using drugs to help you ride the hedge. Here are safer methods to alter your consciousness:

Shamanic drumming works well; you can find many videos on YouTube to help you. There's a start and an ending to the tracks to help you leave this world and gently bring you back to it. Before you use them, you should listen to what they sound like so you know the signal to return to your body. You should limit your ride to 15 minutes initially, and then you can work your way up.

Shamanic music is like drumming, but there are other sounds like chants and rattles. This may not work well for you if you don't like voices.

Rattling is another form of music you can find on YouTube, but it's often better for you to use the rattle to generate the sound. It helps if you sway your body in time with the beat.

Dancing is another method for altering your consciousness, but it's not the easiest, and you can tire easily. The idea is that you must dance until you can no longer remain on your feet. This is ideal when you're dancing around a fire outside or in a warm room with dim lights. If you choose this method, you should have music and chanting to make things go smoothly.

Chanting is similar in effect to drumming and rattling. You can either listen to chants on YouTube or chant on your own. It's often best to work some other action into chanting, like clapping.

Listening to your heartbeat is another option because your heart is basically a biological drum. The room you're in has to be quiet. Take a seat or lie down and then listen to it. You can plug your ears if it helps you hear them better.

Goals

It's a good idea to aim for entering the Lower Realm first. To do this, state your intention to go there out loud. Then repeat the intention in your head over and over again. Then, when you've got that fixed in your head, choose your method for altering your consciousness, and surrender yourself to the process.

When you want to enter the Otherworld, you've got to cross the veil, also known as the hedge. This is a portal, which looks different for every hedge witch. It could be anything from a mirror to a hollowed-out tree trunk. You can bring this image to your mind as you practice your altered state of consciousness technique so that you'll see the portal before you when you switch consciousness.

Go through the portal into a tunnel, which can look like anything, from a hallway of doors to an actual tunnel. If you're going to the Lower Realms, the tunnel should head downwards. The tunnel should be flat when going to the Middle Realms, and the Upper Realms should have a tunnel that leads upward. Keep walking until you finally make your way toward the other side, where there should be light. Please note that this may not happen the very first time you try it. If it doesn't, don't beat yourself up. Just try the next day and the day after that again. Eventually, you will pierce the veil. When you're ready to come back, do so the same way you did.

Ideally, you should get used to the Lower Realms first before you start traveling elsewhere. This is the safest place for you to explore, and when you meet your guides and are familiar with them, you can then move on to the Middle Realms, then the Upper Realms. Please don't set any expectations for yourself so you're not disappointed. As you gain more experience, you will have more interesting journeys. If you have trouble piercing the veil, you may have issues with self-doubt. You need to allow yourself to believe that you can do this and then try again.

Meditation and Deities

Meditation helps you remain grounded and connects you to the deities.
https://www.pexels.com/photo/peaceful-lady-sitting-in-padmasana-pose-while-meditating-on-mat-4498220/

You should be able to work with the deities if you're having difficulty. Just ask for their help by offering them or meditating on them, so you can soak in their energies. Meditation is also a great practice because it helps you remain grounded, which you need when riding the hedge. You can also work with your spirit allies. Who are they? Let's talk about that in the next chapter.

Chapter Five: Spirit Allies and How to Find Them

In this life, you never walk alone. You have a team of supporters who are always with you, regardless of what's happening. You may not be able to see them all the time, but that doesn't mean they're not there. These are your spirit guides or spirit allies. Some beings are devoted to helping you through your life. Your spirit guide(s) could be a power animal, angel, fairy, ancestor, elemental, or entire divine councils.

One important thing to note about your spirit guides is that they must adhere to universal laws. In other words, as much as they may want to help you through a particular situation, they can't interfere unless and until you reach out to them for help. In other words, they are respecters of free will. Your spirit guide is eternally devoted to your highest good. They're there to ensure that you fulfill your soul's calling before you incarnated up on this planet. They're always there to make things easier for you.

Full of compassion and eager to help you, they are in charge of helping to wake you up from the illusion of "real" life. They wake you up to your greatness, so you can see there is no reason to kowtow to the troubles you've been burdened with since you were born. They help you awaken to your innate divinity, showing you areas where you have blind spots. They can teach you the correct attitude to have and help you deal with the daily fears you face. It is well worth it to take some time to learn who your spirit guides are and how they can be of assistance to you. As you do this, you will quickly realize that life doesn't have to be difficult.

Your spirit guide's job is to bring you to places and things that will help you along your journey. They will show you where you're struggling that you may not be aware of and how to break through this struggle. While they are full of love and compassion, they do not have any trouble doing what needs to be done to bring you to where you need to be. They will do everything necessary to make you stop telling the stories you continue to use to imprison yourself in your undesired version of reality. They do this because when you become conscious of who you are, there is nothing that could hold you back from achieving whatever you want in life.

How Your Guides Show Up

Sometimes your spirit guides will reveal themselves in this physical world as very strong supporters of your cause or as people who are incredibly difficult and challenging to deal with. When they show up as the latter, it basically forces you to come face to face with your shadow aspects to heal and integrate them, so you can move on to the next level in life. That very difficult person you're dealing with could be your boss, for instance. Say they continue to assign you duties outside your job description, refuse to give you a raise, or unjustly cut your pay. It's easy to get mad, but there's no reason to. They may not be conscious of this, but your guide could be using them and their constant pushes against you to wake you up to the prison you've constructed and consented to. They could show you it's time to start something new or devote yourself completely to your own business. Your guide could also be working through a lover, showing you the stories you've come to accept about your lack of worth, so you can finally learn that you do deserve love, fully and truly. They can use anyone and any situation to get through to you. You just have to pay attention.

Types of Spirit Guides and How to Connect with Them

Ancestors

These are spirit guides you share a connection with through your physical or spiritual lineage. They could also be some of the people you've known and loved who have passed on to their next life and are now offering you guidance from their higher perspective. It is more common to have your ancestors come from many generations back. They could be a great-grandfather or someone with spiritual gifts who was your former incarnation.

Ancestors are never stingy with their support and guidance. Whether you have limiting beliefs that need to be taken care of or trauma that you need to let go of, they will be there to help you. They can bring your attention to wounds you may have neglected for far too long so you can finally heal them. Sometimes very specific traumas pass on from one generation to the next, which could need healing in your present incarnation. They are also on hand to help you finally help your lineage break free. They can act as teachers, showing you who you really are, and revealing the gifts you may not be aware of so you can use them to live life to the fullest.

How to Connect with Ancestors

1. **Connect with Them through Meditation:** Find a quiet, still space in your home. It can simply be a room where you sit, close your eyes, and meditate. Sit and state your intention to connect with your ancestors out loud, and then keep that intention fixed in your mind while you focus on your breath. Visualize a white light emanating from the top of your head and filling the entire room. Keep this up till you feel the energy shift. This will connect you. From this state, you could let them know what you want them to help you with, express your appreciation for all they've done for you so far, or just let them know you'd like to have a deeper, more meaningful relationship with them.

2. **Start Connecting with Your Elders before They Pass On:** Try to create deep connections with them before they leave this plane, and it will be easier for you to connect with them when they're on the other side in a position to help you more than they possibly could on this side. Don't connect with them only for selfish reasons. Truly be there for them and show them how much you care. They will return the favor from the other side.

3. **Honor Your Family Traditions:** Try to find ways to honor your ancestors. This means participating in some of the traditions you have, whether it be gathering together for family dinners or taking a few moments in your day to say thank you for their advice and wisdom.

4. **Develop a Habit of Speaking to Them Daily:** There is a reason why they want you to connect with them daily. They want to remind you of who you are and help you live your best life by passing on their wisdom, guidance, and teachings. Listen to their call. You want communion with them, which means listening to them, not just talking to them. This way, they will reveal themselves in your life with purpose. But don't be disappointed if they don't always respond right away. Trust that they will, and when the time is right, in a way that works out beautifully for you.

Angels

An angel can be described as a "spirit guide on steroids." They are much more powerful and able to help you in a way that other spirits may not be able to. These beings are of the highest spiritual light and have been here from the beginning of time. The angels are here to help you achieve your highest potential. They help you connect to your spirit, and they can send your messages to the higher realms, making sure they are received. They can help you get into a state of being that is more inspiring than where you're at right now.

Angels are benevolent spiritual beings that help you on your journey. They are not here to judge you; they guide, protect, and heal your soul. They have pure intentions and will not steer you in the wrong direction with what they teach. Angels bring their pure love and light energy in to help you do the things that help guide and assist in your spiritual development.

How to Connect with Angels

1. **Connect with Them through the Act of Prayer:** Prayer is the most common way to connect with your angels. Praying to the angels helps you align your energy with theirs and opens a loving line of communication for when you need them. You can pray for guidance, protection, healing, help with any obstacles in your life, or anything else that's troubling you. A good angel guide to pray to would be Archangel Michael, who is known as the warrior of angelic light and who serves as a mentor to help you in times of trouble.

2. **Notice Intense Sensations and Emotions That Hit You from Nowhere:** These can be flashes of light, a tingling sensation in your body, a sudden wave of energy in your stomach, or any other physical sensation. Your angels may also send you thoughts from out of nowhere.

3. **Intend to Connect with Them in Your Dreams:** You can do this by setting the intention in meditation to connect with your angels during your dream. You can also ask them to help you remember some of your dreams so that you can better understand what they are trying to tell you.

4. **Create a Sacred Space in Your Home:** This is an area where you feel safe, protected, and inspired to connect with higher spiritual beings freely.

Star Beings

Other-dimensional beings heavily influence human life. The star beings have a lot to do with how humanity is today and have helped us get this far regarding our physical and spiritual evolution. You can think of them as our spirit guides from other dimensions, some of whom we know from our past on other planets or in other universes, and others from our future. They have helped us expand our consciousness so we can start to get in touch with other dimensions and beyond.

Star beings are not exactly angels, but they possess similar traits. They also have a lot of knowledge of the future. Their role is to help us further expand our understanding of creation and give us a sense of hope that we will make it through any obstacle or challenge that happens in our life with blessings from other dimensions. The star beings bring higher ideas and notions to Earth and influence how we see things from an entirely new perspective that helps us understand our own spirituality, purpose, and many other factors in life.

How to Connect with Star Beings

1. **Fly the Hedge to Connect with Them:** Each time you fly the hedge, you can set an intention to meet with them or speak with them. You may not do so on the first try, but with patience and with persistence, you'll be able to connect with them. This is because you will have adjusted your vibration to a state where it's easy to connect with them. Note that when you communicate with each other, it will likely be through telepathy. You may experience a phenomenon where you're getting "downloads" of information, which is a much more effective way of getting messages across than with words.

2. **Spend Time Star Gazing:** Observing the stars and other celestial bodies is a great way to connect with higher dimensions. Doing so helps expand your consciousness and gives you a sense of calm and internal peace.

Stargazing helps you connect with star beings.
https://pixabay.com/images/id-1851128/

3. **Meditate:** Through meditating, you work on clearing your mind of any negativity or clutter that may be hindering your ability to connect with star beings. This helps you raise your vibration and get in the right state to connect with them. You may hear their messages through your dreams or just get a general sense of guidance, inspiration, or peace while meditating.

4. **Connect with Them through Crystals:** Crystals have a high concentration of energy that connects with higher dimensions. They can help you connect with the star beings and other spirit guides and allies.

Ascended Masters

They are human beings who incarnated in a past life on Earth to help and teach us along our path. In some cases, they may have incarnated multiple times, but their purpose, for now, is to teach you something, help you with a specific task, or just be there as support for you. Ascended masters may be from other planets or other universes, or they could have been human beings (from Earth) who ascended beyond and experienced countless lifetimes of a tremendous amount of spiritual development throughout many lifetimes.

The ascended masters have spiritually evolved beings who have reached a point of enlightenment, where they are spiritually developed to the point they no longer need reincarnation. They may choose to come back to Earth as an ascended master and help us with our spiritual growth, but the ascension is such that they don't need to experience the suffering and pain of physical life. Some will travel throughout the universe, and others will stay in lower dimensions, but all of them are here on Earth as ascended masters and spirit guides.

How to Connect with Ascended Masters

1. **Open Your Heart to Them:** The ascended masters have reached a point of having an open heart, able to love unconditionally. So, to connect with ascended masters, you need to open your heart to the world. You need to love unconditionally, care for others without putting conditions on them, and get past the fear of being hurt or vulnerable. As you open your heart further, more and more ascended masters will come into your life.

2. **Ask for Help from Ascended Masters:** The ascended masters are compassionate, kind, and selfless beings who are willing to come and help you if you ask them. When you ask for their help, you need to be respectful that their time is precious – just as yours is. If you're asking for guidance on a task or problem in your life, be specific about what you want and respect their time – don't waste it.

3. **Pay Attention to Signs in Your Life:** As you open your heart to others and ask for help, you will begin to see signs and messages from them in the most unlikely places. These signs can be as simple as seeing a butterfly or an owl in a strange place in a strange time or hearing something that reminds you of your goal. Sometimes people report hearing their name being whispered when nobody is around. Some people have reported seeing an image of themselves from the future because they can connect with their future self using their higher intuition.

4.**Meditate on Your Higher Self:** You may find connecting with your higher self easier than the masters. You may also be closer to what is your higher self than even spiritual masters or angels since your higher self is the most evolved form of yourself and is closer to God. When you meditate on your higher self, you can ask it to put you in touch with the masters if you want, and it will be easier.

Animal Spirit Guides

Animal spirit guides are spiritual or angelic beings that can take many animal forms and are an extension of yourself. You're meant to connect with them and the Divine through them. Like ascended masters, animal spirit guides may have incarnated in a past life on Earth for a reason, but in this time, they work with you to help you awaken spiritually.

These are animal guides who have been with us since birth. Although they may not seem like much, they are extremely powerful, intelligent, and wise beings who can teach you many things about yourself. Who we are as human beings is a combination of our personality and our animal spirit guides.

How to Connect with Animal Spirit Guides

1.**Connect with Your Senses:** Animals are very in touch with their senses, and so it makes sense that you connect with yours if you want to relate to them. So, practice really looking around, taking in everything around you. Notice what you can hear and the different qualities in each sound. Pay attention to what you can smell, feel, and taste. Work with each sense one at a time for five minutes a day.

2.**Get a Talisman That Represents the Animal You're Most Drawn to:** A talisman is an object that has a spiritual significance. You can carry your talisman with you everywhere and connect with it whenever you're having trouble. Talismans are medallions or objects which have been charged with the energy of a specific time and place, as well as being imbued with the universal energy of creation. To charge your talisman, you can meditate on your preferred animal while you hold the talisman in your hands and set an intention so that, as you carry it around with you, you have the guidance, protection, and assistance of your spirit animal wherever you are.

3. **Connect with Them in Your Dreams:** Our dreams are the best place to reconnect with our animal spirit guides. These beings are very powerful in dreams, and some report having lucid dreams or daydreaming about them. All you have to do is set the intention to meet with them as you go to sleep.

4. **Ask Them for Help:** You can ask your animal spirit guides for anything. This is a great way to learn more about yourself and discover your purpose on Earth. Don't be surprised if you start seeing or hearing about that animal more often when you reach out for help. When they show up, they're trying to tell you everything will be okay and that they are working on what you want.

Deities

We've already talked about some deities particular to hedge witchcraft and Celtic lore. You can connect with anyone you resonate with, and they will answer you. Just make sure to be respectful of them and their time and be sincere in whatever you want to ask for their assistance.

How to Connect with Deities

1. **Make Offerings to Them:** You know what it is they like. Offer it to them by setting it on your altar.

2. **Set Their Image around Your Space:** You can have pictures of your deities in your home or around your spiritual workspace. Each time you see the picture, take a moment to say hello in your mind, thank them, or just acknowledge them however you can.

3. **Light a Candle in Their Honor:** If you're feeling lost, depressed, anxious, or even very happy because something good happened, you can light a candle to acknowledge them. This practice will fill your home and life with their energy.

4.**Meditate on Them**: You can chant their name repeatedly as you meditate, either aloud or in your mind. As you do this, you'll feel your body and heart filled with their energy. That tells you that they're present with you.

Elemental Spirit Guides

Elementals are spirits that you find in one of the four classical elements: Earth, water, fire, and air. Not all of them are allies, but the ones who are can be considered guides. Gnomes are earth elementals, undines are connected to water, pyraustas are also known as salamanders, and they're connected to fire, while sylphs are connected to water. Generally, these elementals will make their home in the elements themselves, like rocks, mountains, bodies of water, fire, and the wind.

How to Connect with Elemental Spirit Guides

1.**Spend Time in Nature:** The more you are out in nature, the more you'll be able to connect with them.

2.**Start Caring for the Planet:** You can do this by becoming more conscious about your habits and practices that don't do our earth any favors. You can also do little things like getting rid of litter, raking leaves, etc. As you do these things, keep the elements in your mind.

3.**Intend to Connect with Them:** This is easy to do when you're working with a specific element. Air is all around you, so you should have no problem with that. It might help to go camping or at least light a candle for fire. For water, you can work with a bowl full of it. As for the earth, sand or salt will do.

4.**Carry around the Element You Want to Work With:** It can be a bit trickier for fire and air, but for the former, you can just use a lighter or a match. For the latter, becoming conscious of the air you're breathing will do the trick.

The Aos Si

These are like elves or fairies, coming from the Tuatha Dé Danann. They make their home underground in a world that, while invisible, exists right along with ours. They are immortal, and they can help you in life as well. Some people call them The Fair Folk, while others call them The Good Neighbors, and they are exactly that. They can be as hideous as they are stunning in how they look. They act as guardians, fiercely protective of those they consider theirs.

How to Connect with the Aos Si

1. **Fly the Hedge:** This is a good way to reach them, as they're essentially inhabitants of the Otherworld.

2. **Meditate on Them at Dawn and Dusk:** These are the two periods when the veil between worlds is thinnest, and therefore you should find it easier to connect with them and let them know what you need them to help with.

3. **Celebrate Their Holidays:** Now's a good time to get familiar with Midsummer, Beltane, and Samhain. These are the three festivals with which they are most associated. You can work with fellow hedge witches to make them group offerings. The combined energies will prove to be fruitful, regardless of what you seek from them.

4. **Offer Them Foods Regularly:** Berries, apples, milk, and other baked goods are a favorite for the Good Neighbors.

Chapter Six: Magical Herbs, Plants, and Trees

In this chapter, we'll talk about the magical herbs, plants, and trees you can work with in your craft. You can easily pick up all these herbs from your grocery store or a store that sells items for witchcraft. You can also find them online, fresh or dried, so there's no need to be obsessed with scouting around your neighborhood looking for them unless that's something you like to do.

Magical Herbs

Mint: It's kind of odd to have mint included as a magical herb to some witches, but the truth is that it is powerful and deserves to be mentioned. This herb can give you energy and add power to your rituals and spells. It will help you clear your mind and set intentions to bring proper results. It also awakens your senses, which is always good for magical work. You can drink it as tea, eat it, or just smell it to prime yourself to do your spells successfully. This herb can also draw success and money to you, and it's good for drumming up business. Good spirits are attracted to it, and it keeps your home safe from negative energies and entities.

Thyme: This herb is popular in various spells because it has so many intriguing properties and uses. You can use thyme if you want to speak with the dead and connect with them. It's also good for consecrating rituals and keeping your spells aligned with your intentions. You can wear it to ward off snakes and spiders, keep it around the house to protect your family from illness, or add a bit of thyme to your bath water for a relaxing soak. Be sure that you're planting organic thyme, though. No one wants pesticides in their "magical" herb garden.

Bay Leaf: You can use this leaf to hold divine energy. It's a very versatile herb and works for various types of spells and magical workings. If you're trying to cleanse your aura, wear it in a pendant or amulet. If you want to ask your deity to bless you, you can burn its leaves in incense. It will also help you with spells that involve protection, luck, and prosperity because it's an herb of abundance. It is especially useful in protection and cleansing rites. It's a good herb for removing negative entities and cleansing your space. You can use the bay leaf in your bath water to cleanse yourself of "negative energies." Bay leaves are also great for drawing good luck and attracting prosperity.

Rosemary: Rosemary is one of the oldest herbs on earth, and its scent is magnificent. You can use it in incense for purification and blessings. Burning it is also a great way to attract good energy into your home or workplace. Rosemary is a very versatile herb, and it's good for healing in various ways. It's also a potent herb for protection magic, and its scent adds an energy vibration that can help you focus your intent. Burning rosemary at night will keep the evil spirits away from you and your family. You can also rub the leaves on your body to prevent illness or add some sprigs to your bath water for a relaxing soak.

Rosemary attracts healing.
https://pixabay.com/images/id-1140763/

Lavender: Lavender is a lovely smelling herb that has many magical uses. You can use it to cleanse yourself before entering a sacred space or performing magic. It's also good for ritual work and as a repellent for unwanted spirits. It can remove negative energy or change its vibration. Burn it in an incense burner for attraction magic, or sprinkle some around your house to repel unwanted entities. Wear it in jewelry, put some on the bottom of your feet before you go out, leave a bundle under your bed, or place a lavender sachet in your car, so you'll be protected as you go about town.

Oregano: These leaves are great for drawing good luck and attracting prosperity. They stimulate the senses and clear the mind so you can set proper intentions. Add some to salads or put a few pinches in your ritual bath. Oregano is also used in shamanic practices to help you connect with the spirit world. During ritual work, burn it in an incense burner or grind a few leaves and add them to your bath water. You can also sprinkle it around your home for protection or wear it as an amulet for added safety when traveling.

Ginger Root: This herb is great for healing and exorcism. It can also help you stay focused during spell work and ritual work. It's a powerful blocker against negative thoughts and actions, so it helps you keep your intentions pure. When magical work is done around the house, burn some ginger in an incense burner or sachet to clear out the energy from the space, or wear it as a pendant to ward off negativity and attract good fortune. Ginger root is great for drawing; good luck to you. It's also wonderful for adding energy to many types of rituals, spells, and magic work, as it acts as a magical accelerant. It's great for banishing spirits and removing negative energy from your space. Ginger root will also lift your spirits and help you feel more energetic during your spells and rituals.

Fennel Seed: Fennel seed is a powerful herb used in ritual work. It has a sweet scent that acts as a stimulant for the mind, so you can use it in spells to keep you focused on your intentions. This herb is also very good for purification magic because it cleanses the aura of negative energy, which is good for any spell or ritual that involves protection, health, or cleanliness issues.

Allspice: This is another herb that witches can use in many rituals. It is an excellent purifying agent, is used against negativity, and helps you communicate with the dead. The smell is reminiscent of clove and cinnamon, and the taste also hints of black pepper. It's a very popular addition to feast offerings to the gods and goddesses. Allspice can be used in any magic, from blessing rituals to protection magic. It is also considered a sacred herb by many cultures. You can use it in spells involving love, money, and fertility.

Dandelion: Dandelion is one of the most popular magical herbs because it's both easy and inexpensive to obtain. The root is used in magical arts to remove negativity, while the leaves and flowers attract abundance. You can also use this herb during spells that involve home protection, luck, love, and purification. It's a very potent spell enhancer that improves the power of any spell or magic you perform with it. To attract money, burn dandelion on charcoal for your incense, or put some in a sachet for travel money or business earnings. Dandelion is a great herb that can be used as a tea, too. Traditionally, this herb is also used for healing.

It's good to sprinkle it on the ground where you practice your craft or wear it as an amulet before entering your ritual area.

Magical Plants

Money Tree: This herb has so many desirable qualities that it's used in almost every type of magic, from blessing rituals to protection spells and love rituals. In some cultures, the leaves are used as an ingredient in lucky tea or herbal brews consumed to draw good fortune and prosperity. You can use it in any spell that brings good fortune or prosperity your way. Try pairing it with other herbs like ginger, cinnamon, or nutmeg for added effect.

Jade Plant: This plant represents abundance and energy. It is a good one to use when you want wisdom. You can make a protective sachet of jade and carry it with you as you travel to ward off unwanted energies. You can use jade to lift your spirits when feeling down or stressed. This plant is also good for clearing out negativity in the aura, so it's a great helper when working on spells that involve the mind or emotions. This is a magical herb that's used in rituals and spells involving psychic awareness, as well as healing properties. It is known to bring good luck and to help you achieve your goals. You can also use it in household cleansing spells.

Devil's Ivy: This herb is traditionally used in magic to attract prosperity, but it can also be used to draw luck. When you use devil's ivy, it brings goodwill and fortune and strengthens your powers of perception. Devil's ivy is also excellent for protecting your home or property. It's a good herb for making love potions or for healing spells. Devil's ivy has a very powerful scent that repels all the negative energy in the area. You can use it to purify your space or in protection and health spells. Wearing the plant as an amulet will help you ward off many types of negativity, including thoughts and physical harassment. Use this plant to give you resilience and to help you work spells that involve forgiveness.

English Ivy: This popular magical herb is used to protect magic, increase psychic powers, and promote goodwill. It's a very good one to use in spells involving cleansing and protection. You can also use it in spells that involve banishing negativity or evil. English ivy is easy to find, inexpensive, and easy to grow - all of which make this one of the most popular magical herbs around. You can use it in any type of protective or blessing spell. Because the scent is both sweet and fragrant, it's a good herb to banish negative thoughts and attract positive energy into your life.

Houseleek: This plant is a succulent one also called Hens and Chicks. It's underrated but powerful. The ancient Romans would decorate their homes with this plant. You can eat it, but only in small amounts. It's great if you want to deal with inflammation in the body. Use this plant to create good health in your life. It can also improve your family affairs, boost fertility in whatever aspect of life you need it, and keep you protected. This plant gives off a comforting aura, putting you at ease and turning anywhere it grows into a home. You can also use them to bring more sexual energy into the bedroom or with spells that involve love and sexuality.

Bamboo: This is a good herb to use for purification and protection magic. It represents money and sexuality. Bamboo can attract money, wealth, and power when burned as incense or used in spellwork. Bamboo represents resilience and flexibility. It also promotes peace and clarity and can bring you good luck. Bamboo's smooth branches are sometimes used for spiritual cleansing and meditation as a tool for divination. You can use it to attract happiness and health into your life. It is said that the more stalks of this plant you have, the more power and luck you can draw on for your craft.

Magical Trees

Alder: Many ancient people considered the alder tree to be sacred. It was used in many magical and religious rituals because it is so very powerful. This tree is beneficial for protection spells, cleansing rites, and healing magic. It's also used for banishing evil spirits and negative energies, and it can help you boost your psychic powers and strengthen your memory. You can use its parts for ritual work or spells involving the banishment of negativity, healing, meditation, and communication with spirits. Use it as part of a protective mojo bag or scatter some leaves around the area where you're doing your spell or ritual work so that the energy will feel welcoming and positive.

Beech: This tree is a wonderful source of spiritual energy because its wood has been used in making ritual tools since the Stone Age. It's used in divination and has been associated with gods and goddesses since ancient times. It can help you focus your psychic abilities, so it's great for spell work involving divination or any type of clairvoyance. Beech can also attract love, peace, and happiness or dial up the power of your spells. It also reduces stress, so it's perfect for protective amulets or talismans you want to carry with you during travels. A piece of beech wood will also help you keep your own energy private.

Oak: The oak is a powerful tree that helps you stay grounded during magic rituals and spell work. If you need to focus on something to straighten out karma, this is your tree. Its branches are used to make wands, and its leaves help call forth spirits and elemental energies. Oak is also good to use when cleansing your negative energy space. Oak is often carved and used as an altar tool during ceremonial magic. Its branches are also used to create magical tools, and its leaves were used for divination by the Celts.

Willow: Willow can be used to protect spells and stop evil spirits from harming you or your loved ones. It's also very helpful during magical protection if you want to direct the protection efforts of other trees or herbs. Willow is also widely used in healing magic, particularly in pain and discomfort. It can help relieve physical pain and provides relief from emotional pain. You can burn it in the same room as your altar or wear it to dispel bad luck.

White Oak Tree: This tree is sacred to magic rituals because of its associations with the Goddess energies. The ancient Egyptians also used it for various purposes, including treating eye problems, earaches, and headaches. White oak will help you raise your power so you can project your intentions outwards and bring about positive changes in the world around you.

Witch Hazel: The leaves and bark of this plant are used to create a magical force that is used in spells and rituals to attract love, abundance, and happiness. It's also good for protection magic, so if you're doing spell work around the house, put some in your ritual bath or wear it as an amulet to keep the forces of darkness away from you. Burn hazel on an incense burner to eliminate negative energy in your home or workspace. It's also good for meditation and for strengthening intuitive powers.

Rowan: To the Celts, the rowan tree represented rebirth, protection, and good fortune. It was also a sacred tree of the Norse. It can help you increase your connection with the spirits, so it's a fantastic herb or tree to burn during rituals or spells where you're trying to reach out to the other side. Rowan is often used in rituals to protect homes and ward off negativity. It's also used in money and health spells designed to improve digestion and relieve stomach issues.

Chapter Seven: Hedge Divination

Divination involves being able to investigate the past and the future to get answers. Hedge witchcraft is a very adaptive practice, which means there are lots of divination techniques you could choose from. Let's look at each one in detail.

Tea Reading

Tea leaf reading is a common method of divination.
_https://commons.wikimedia.org/wiki/File:Tea_leaf_reading.jpg_

Since the dawn of time, people have been practicing divination. One of the most common methods is tea reading, also called tasseomancy. It's from a marriage of two words: Tassa, an Arabic word that translates to "cup," and Mancy, a Greek word that refers to divination itself.

European diviners during the medieval era would do all their readings by working with wax or lead splatters. However, tea soon became very popular, and so it naturally became a part of the divination process. You can choose to work with special cups for this process. Often, they'll have some magical symbols etched around the body or rim to help you with interpretation.

How to Read Tea Leaves

To read tea leaves, you'll have to brew a cup of tea, but unlike a regular cup, you're not going to strain out the leaves. Choose a teacup with a light color so it's easy for you to see what's happening at the bottom of the cup. When it comes to the tea you choose, you can work with any type you want. The only caveat is that they must be the loose-leaf kind. You want larger leaves because they're much easier for you to read. If you want to be specific about the kind of tea you choose, go for Earl Grey, as it has large, loose leaves. You could also work with Darjeeling. The Indian tea blends, while delicious, aren't the best for divination purposes because sometimes they have very fine particles, little twigs, and much smaller leaves.

When you or the seeker has finished drinking the tea, all you should have left in the cup are the leaves at the bottom of the cup. Give the cup a swirl three times, and then set the cup down and allow the contents to settle. The leaves will form a pattern which you can then interpret. You can work with symbols that are well known, having been handed down through generations. For instance, the leaves from an apple could mean education or knowledge. If it looks like a dog, it could mean "loyalty." A quick search on the Internet will show you the signs you can work with and their meanings. Keep in mind that just because you see a dog doesn't mean there's someone who is loyal. It could be a sign of the complete opposite. It all comes down to context and what your intuition is telling you.

Speaking of intuition, you can work with that instead of setting symbolic meanings. Just allow the leaves to speak to your spirit while you pass on the message to the querent. It's a good idea to get some practice with friends and family first so that you're sure you're on point more often than you aren't. Sit with the leaves, and as you look at them, pay attention to the feelings they drum up in you. Do you feel something positive or negative? What aspects of life are coming into your mind right now? Check in with the seeker to help you fine-tune the message from the leaves.

Keep in mind that sometimes you'll see more than one image. You could have a prominent image in the middle surrounded by smaller ones, or they could all be about the same size. Whatever you do, begin with the images from the cup's handle and then move around the cup in a clockwise manner. Are you working with a handle-less cup? Then start from the noon position (up north) and work your way clockwise around the cup.

Please make sure you keep notes as you read the leaves. Take pictures with your phone so you don't have to worry about accidentally upsetting the positions of the leaves. Pay attention to the first thing you notice because this is the most profound piece of information the divine is trying to communicate with you. Sometimes you may not get images but numbers or letters. You may also see ancient or alien symbols or even animal shapes.

Finally, divide the cup into different parts because placing the symbols or images is also important. The rim stands for matters that concern the here and now. The center is about the immediate future, which could be anywhere from seven days to a month. The bottom of the cup holds the key to your situation as a whole in the present.

Full Moon Scrying

Scrying is about looking into a reflective surface and allowing it to reveal the truth to you about the past, present, or future. It's commonly done with water, a crystal ball, or even a mirror. In the Egyptian Book of the Dead, you will find mentions of the process of scrying, especially regarding using Hathor's mirror to see what the future holds. The ancient Romans were no strangers to this, either. Before Christianity was introduced to the Celts, they would use crystals like beryl to learn about the future. Even the great Nostradamus practiced water scrying with candlelight to learn what he had to.

However, if you want to really draw more power into the process, working with the full moon is the way to go. The full moon represents intuition and has an aura of wisdom about it. We sense this deeply, which is why we feel so alive when the moon is at its fullest. This is because we have a connection with the lunar cycle.

You can do this indoors, but it's better outside because you're going to work with the reflection of the full moon's light on the water. It's best to work on the night of the full moon itself, but if you can't, you can do this on the night after or before. You'll need the sky to be clear.

How to Do Full Moon Scrying
You'll Need:

- A dark bowl
- A table or your altar
- A pitcher of water
- A journal and a pen

Steps:

1. Cast a circle by sprinkling salt on the floor around yourself and your altar. You should be barefoot.
2. Shut your eyes and pay attention to how you feel. Pay attention to the energy of the world around you as well. Become one with the sounds, smells, and feelings.
3. Now, turn your inner awareness to the moonlight. Feel its power flowing through you. Know and accept that you're connected to this power and therefore connected to the Universe.
4. When you feel ready, open your eyes and notice the night and its sights. You should be feeling very alert and grounded. This is the moon's power flowing through you.
5. Raise your pitcher and imagine that the water is full of the moon's wisdom as you pour it into the bowl. Imagine

that the moonlight is charging the water even more with its energy. Fill the bowl, then set your pitcher down.

6. Stand over the bowl to keep your shadow from blocking the moonlight reflecting on the water.

7. Stare into the water. Don't strain to see images. Let them come on their own. You may see words or actual pictures or scenes on the water. Also, you may have ideas and concepts popping into your mind. Note everything you see and think down in a journal. You can stare into the water for a few minutes or hours.

8. If the messages don't make sense immediately, that's fine, and they could make more sense over the coming days. The message may pertain to you or to someone close to you.

9. Use the water to work more magic later, or water your plants with it.

Note that you can perform this scrying method with a lake or a river instead of a water bowl.

Pendulum Divination

Working with pendulums is one of the easiest ways to learn what you want from the divine. All you're doing is asking yes or no questions and then waiting for an answer. You can make your own pendulum or just buy an already made one. If you're going to make yours, you can work with any object that has weight. A stone or a crystal is great. You will also need a string or jeweler's wire and a light chain. Wrap the jeweler's wire around the stone and, at the top, create a loop. Put one end of your light chain through the loop. The chain must be long enough to allow you to swing the stone but not so long that you find it keeps bumping into things. Make sure you file off or tuck in the wire bits that stick out, so you don't hurt yourself.

When you've finished, it's time to charge your pendulum. Just put it in some salt water overnight. Please be sure that the stone you're working with can handle salt and water. Otherwise, you can just bury it underground overnight or let it absorb moonlight overnight.

After this, it's time to carry out calibration. Basically, you want to know what your pendulum does when it means yes and no. Hold on to the chain and let the stone hang, keeping your forearm balanced on a table for stability. Then ask an obvious yes or no question, such as, "Is my name Gary?" If it is, you should see it swing back and forth or side to side as *yes*. Ask another question that would yield you a no, then another that gives you a yes. Ask a couple more questions, and you should know what it means. Note that sometimes you may get circular movement instead, and other times your pendulum may not respond. When you've calibrated it, you can finally ask it whatever questions you want.

How to Use Your Pendulum for Divination

You will need to ask only yes or no questions, but you shouldn't let that make you feel limited because you can learn a lot from the right questions. You can work with a divination board, which has letters on it. It's almost like an Ouija board, as it has numbers and letters and words, maybe, no, and yes. You can also use your pendulum as a dowsing rod to help you find missing things. Move around the room you suspect the item is in and note if your pendulum moves faster (meaning you're close to it) or slower (meaning you're far from it). If you need to find something but only know the country or building, you can use a list of each state, a map, a list of each room, or the building's schematics. Let the pendulum hover over each place and pay attention to the one it seems most excited about as it moves. You could incorporate tarot cards if you want answers that require much more than a simple yes or no. Use the pendulum to lead you to the card, which you can then interpret as needed.

The Celtic Ogham

The word Ogham is from the name of the Celtic god Ogmios or Ogma. He's in charge of granting literacy and eloquence to one and all. The Ogham staves have letters of the Ogham alphabet and are used as divination tools for those who choose to practice their hedge craft the Celtic way. There were 20 letters in the Ogham alphabet; later, that number went up to 25. All the letters match up to a sound and represent a specific tree or wood. They also represent various aspects of what it means to be human.

If you want to, you can create your very own Ogham staves. All you need is to find twigs that are the same lengths or cut them into the same length. You'll need 26 of them, with the last one being the blank one. Ideally, each twig should be anywhere from 4 to 6 inches. Using sandpaper, smooth out the twigs and carve in the Ogham symbols on each, one symbol per twig. You can also paint them on if you prefer.

When you've finished, consider the meaning of each symbol. Sit with each one in meditation, soaking in their aura and unique interpretations. You should be able to feel the magic of each symbol. Make sure you're in the right headspace for this and that you will not be distracted. After this, consecrate the staves by asking your preferred deity for help, and then you can go ahead to work with the staves. To do this, keep them in a bag, then consider what you want to know. Stick your hand in the bag, give the staves a good shuffle, and then pull one out. The following is the Ogham alphabet and what each letter means:

Beth or Beith: Birch, new beginnings, rebirth, release, purification, change, hardiness, releasing of negative energies, learning of toxic habits, discovering toxic relationships, letting go of toxicity, a need to focus on the positive, time for emotional and spiritual regeneration, fruitfulness after hard times.

Luis: Rowan, blessings, protection, wisdom, insight, high awareness, intuition, trust, staying true to spiritual nature, staying grounded when unsure.

Fearn or Fern: Alder, the evolution of spirit, spring equinox, March, Bran, hardiness, perseverance, individuality, appreciation for others' uniqueness, mediation, instinct, wise counsel, the voice of reason.

Sallie or Suil: Willow, rapid growth, nourishment, April, healing, protection, moon cycles, female mysteries, female cycles, pain relief, flexibility, adaptability, openness to change, acceptance of unpleasant lessons for spiritual growth, the need to take a break, spiritual rest, trust in coming change, call for flexibility in spiritual matters.

Nionor Nin: Ash, the connection of the world within and the world without, creativity, sacrifice for higher goals, wisdom, consequences, spiritual interconnection, and the balance between the natural and supernatural.

Huath or Uathe: Hawthorn, defense, protection, cleansing, Beltane, fire, masculine energy, fertility, virility, the Fae, successful child conception, health, spiritual strength, overcoming problems, guidance, being a strength for others to draw on.

Duir or Dair: Oak, self-confidence, resilience, strength, domination, summer, doorways, success, money, fertility, good fortune, masculinity, durability, health, prevailing against difficulties, and unpredictability.

Tinne or Teine: Holly, evergreen, courage, immortality, home, hearth, stability, unity, protection, change, transition, blessing, a call to listen to intuition, quick response, adaptability to new situations, triumph, trust for instinct, the balance of logic and desire.

Coll or Call: Hazel, August, hazel moon, life force, creativity, wisdom, knowledge, divination, sacred waters, self-defense, using what you have, sharing what you know, seeking inspiration, allowing oneself to be led by the divine, working with art, receiving more inspiration.

Squirt or Ceirt: Apple tree, faithfulness, rebirth, love, magic, life's never-ending cycle, fertility, prosperity, the need to make the right choice, openness to new paths, receiving spiritual gifts, allowing things to not make sense.

Muin: Vines, wine, prophecy, truth, pausing before speaking, honesty, divination, moderation in life's pleasures.

Gort: Ivy, searching for yourself, wildness, growth, mysticism, evolution, spiritual development, Samhain, October, rebirth, death, life, good fortune for women, protection from magic, protection from curses, love, the banishment of all negative things and relationships, seeking answers from within, looking outside for spiritual allies.

Ng or nGeatal: Reed, purpose, action, health, healing, friends and family, leadership, rebuilding what's been torn down, bringing order back, proactivity over-reactivity, spiritual growth.

St or Straith or Straif: Blackthorn, control authority, triumph over enemies, strength, dark magic, the Morrigan, the Crone, expecting the unexpected, accepting change in plans, external influence, the start of a new journey, pleasant and unpleasant surprises to come.

Ruis: Elder, winter, endings, awareness from experience, maturity, rejuvenation, recovery, the Goddess, the Fae, preservation, transition, knowledge, maturity, a call to be childlike rather than childish, newness.

Ailim or Ailm: Elm, perspective, vision, Beltane, flexibility, the big picture, long-term goals, preparation, noting your progress, spiritual growth, wisdom, and others' inspiration and help.

Onn or Ohn: Gorse bush, long-term plans, determination, hope, perseverance, banishing the bad, manifesting desire, using your gifts to bless others, mentorship, leadership.

Ura or Uhr: Heather, generosity, passion, spiritual messengers, the Otherworld, assurance of victory, time to de-stress, physical, mental, and spiritual healing.

Eadhadh or Eadha: Courage, endurance, durability, success, strong will, triumph over enemies and stumbling blocks, protection, the Fae, bending but not breaking, adversity about to end, releasing of fear, allowing yourself to be vulnerable, focusing on your spiritual growth, taking the first step.

Iodhadh or Idad: Yew, Endings, death, new from the old, rebirth, major changes to come, time to release what doesn't serve, taking advantage of major transitions.

Eabhadh: Grove trees, conflict resolution, wise counsel, justice, spiritual harmony, clearing of misunderstandings, need for communication, leading by example, less talk, and more action, fairness, wisdom, and ethics.

Oi or Oir: Spindle, strength in vulnerability, family honor, fulfilling obligations, curiosity, connection to others.

Uillean: Honeysuckle, manifesting your desire, secret wants, goals, finding who you are, freedom to go after what you want, fulfilling dreams, enjoying life, holding on to values, uncovering mysteries.

Ifin or Iphin: Pine, vision, clear conscience, the need to stop feeling guilty, time to make amends, time to move on, being intellectual instead of emotional.

Amhancholl or Eamhancholl: Hazel, cleansing, purifying, releasing emotional baggage, releasing stale energies, reevaluating spiritual journey, rethinking priorities.

Chapter Eight: Kitchen Magic

Hedge witches have been around for centuries and have learned the magic of using their cooking skills in many ways. What hedge witches typically practice is known as kitchen magic. Kitchen magic can be practiced by anyone interested in it, regardless of their spirituality or belief system. Whether you are looking to make new friends while feeding your community or joining a coven that shares your pagan beliefs, this chapter will help you get started on practicing kitchen magic as an everyday hedge witch.

Kitchen Magic is fun and powerful. It all starts from the hearth, which is where the entire home is fueled from. It's a practice that is very ancient, practiced by females who were well aware of the power of plants and herbs and who knew how to channel that power to achieve different effects, from healing and blessing to protection from the evil eye.

A kitchen is a place in the home with many superstitions and stories. Originally, the hearth was fashioned to make offerings to the divine and partake of these offerings. Where others only see ingredients for cooking, the kitchen witch can see and feel the magic waiting to be put to good use. You could think of the process of kitchen magic as being like meditation, where everything that's done in the kitchen, from cooking to cleaning, is imbued with magical intention.

Like several other types of magic, kitchen magic can be used for good or bad purposes. The recipes you will find in this chapter are examples of good kitchen magic. You can transform your kitchen into a place of alchemy, where you are the magician who can mix ingredients to produce magic results and create wonderful dishes that delight the senses and have numerous magical properties.

Your kitchen magic doesn't have to be limited to food. You can use your cooking skills and knowledge of kitchen magic to create some amazing candles and other paraphernalia. Try mixing all-natural ingredients, like beeswax, soy wax, and essential oils to make scented candles. There are hundreds of different recipes for making these natural candles online. You can also use kitchen magic for more practical purposes by making your own laundry detergent or cleaning products.

No one's a better hostess than the hedge witch who works kitchen magic. You can trust that everything in her kitchen is a magical tool. She can wield her steak knife as a boline or an athame. She can use a carrot as a wand. It doesn't matter what she works with. What matters is the attitude she pursues her craft with, so if you want to practice, you should consider your home a sacred space.

What Kitchen Witches Do

A kitchen witch can grow her own herbs if she wants to. She can work with them to help bless others or perform a much-needed cleansing. She can also practice tasseomancy to help her guests, whip up a special brew of tea to help you if you've got a nasty cold or a case of the blues, and much more. As a hedge witch, you're also a kitchen witch if you choose to work magic with your food. You don't need to subscribe to a certain faith or let your religious leanings keep you away from your craft, either. You'll know if you have a penchant for kitchen magic based on how you approach cooking. If you have a passion for whipping up good meals and love when others enjoy your cooking, you're not too far away from becoming a kitchen witch yourself. All you need is some magical intent.

So, You Think You're a Kitchen Witch, Too?

A kitchen witch is also called a *cottage witch*; her spells are her magical meals. You can work with deities or spirits as you cook to draw on their energy and make your spells even more powerful. If you find that you're drawn to kitchen magic but don't know where to begin, the first thing you should do is keep things simple. This form of magic is very practical and to the point. What's going to change in how you cook is you will bring more mindfulness and intention to every part of the process. Because you do this, you're also going to notice that the way you think of your home and personal space will also change.

Your countertop and stove will both serve as your altar, so you can put the spiritual items that remind you of what you want to achieve with your magic onto them. Also, you want to set up your home so that when people come in, they feel relaxed, like they're escaping the world's harsh realities.

You may want to take up some gardening, as it's a great thing to have fresh herbs on hand for whatever meal you want to prepare. All you need is a window ledge with enough sunlight to grow your herbs. As a bonus, growing plants in your home brings lovely, magical energy. If you can't grow herbs or aren't interested, that's fine too. You can work with dry options; just because they're dry doesn't mean they've lost their potency.

According to traditions and lore, you should also do your homework on what each herb and plant you're working with represents. Check out the significance of each kitchen tool and action as well. For instance, when sweeping dirt off your floor, you should empty it outside the home to allow more good fortune into your space and your life. So, the next time you do this, being more mindful of the spiritual implication guarantees you will draw in good fortune.

Setting Up the Space

Your altar shouldn't have clutter on it, so take care if that's the case. Use your hands or a magic broom to sweep away all stale, stuck, negative energies still hovering around the space when it's all gone. On your altar, put some statues or symbols that represent the energies and beings you want to work your craft with. You can have general ones or specific ones for particular spells you want to cast.

You should also place the tools you'll often use on your altar, like utensils, spoons, chopsticks, your pestle and mortar, knives, athame, wand, and so on. You'll also need to have your grimoire handy, so you can refer to the spells you've got in them or make notes as needed about what you're doing differently with the spell you're working on. You can also place your sacred herbs and other foods here. Let's not forget you'll need your cauldron. You don't have to use it, though, as it could just be symbolic. You get to figure out what's the best option for you.

Working with Deities

You don't have to devote yourself to one deity over another. You can work with several to make different spells. For instance, if you want to make a lucky meal, working with Fortuna is a good idea. She is the goddess of all fortune. Another goddess you can work with is Annapurna, who oversees food and nourishment according to the Hindus. Anna means "food," and *Purna* means full or complete. She makes sure that we have sustenance. According to lore, her consort, Shiva, once declared that males were the superior gender. So, Annapurna disappeared in her anger and, as a result, the world was plunged into a terrible famine. Everyone was saved only when she decided to return and share her bounty with the world. Working with her will bless your spells.

You could also work with Andhrimnir. He is the Aesir Gods' chef. Lore has it that each day, he heads out to slaughter Saehrimnir the boar, and then he cooks it to offer to the Gods. Each night, Saehrimnir comes back to life. Andhrimnir is good to work with because he is an amazing cook, and so if you want to do better and give your loved ones a meal they won't forget in a hurry, work with him.

Hestia, the Greek goddess of the hearth, is another deity who can help you. She's all about family, warmth, love, and food. According to lore, Hestia was the one Zeus trusted to make sure the Olympus fire wouldn't burn out. She did this by offering fatty meat to be burned as a sacrifice. Work with her, and you'll have meals that strengthen the connection between everyone under your roof or taking part in eating the meal.

Crafting Magical Spells

While every ingredient in the meal is magical by virtue of you acknowledging that, the key knowledge you need to understand surrounds the spices and herbs and their energy properties. When you understand their powers, you can simply add the relevant herb to your meal to make it magical. Here's a quick list of the basic spices and herbs you will be working with and what they bring to the table, magically speaking:

- **Rosemary:** Good for improving memory, encouraging clear thought, protection, and boosting strength and courage. Also, good for blessing.

- **Allspice:** Excellent for energy, happiness, peace, and success.

- **Cinnamon:** Increases psychic powers, gives success, and promotes healing.

- **Ginger:** Acts as an energy enhancer and accelerates the speed of your spell's manifestation. Also, good for power, money, and love spells.

- **Coriander:** Use this for money and health matters.

- **Cloves:** Used for purification, protection, and success.

- **Basil:** Boosts creativity, inspires courage, and is great for protection. Also brings you abundance, good luck, psychic power, lust, and love.

- **Bay leaves:** Wisdom, divination, prosperity, protection, love, and joy.

- **Garlic:** Excellent for protection from negative energies. Also, good for attaining power.

- **Parsley:** Add this to your spells for purification.

- **Mint:** Use to draw in success, love, money, and lust. Encourages happiness, peace, and safety.

Mint encourages happiness.

- **Nutmeg:** Use this for intuition and psychic growth. Also, use it to encourage peace, happiness, and prosperity.

- **Sage:** For spiritual wisdom, divination, protection, purification, longevity, courage, wealth, and prosperity in all your affairs.

Kitchen Magic Recipes

You'll use several ingredients with different magical properties when you cook a meal. The trick here, therefore, is to focus your attention and energy on manifesting the properties of the specific ingredients you want to use. Some people have recipes like "Bye Bad Luck Pie" or "Feel Better Veggie Soup," but the truth is that the same pie or soup can be used for other purposes than warding off bad luck or making someone feel better because there are other ingredients in them.

So, think about your intention for your spell, then consider the herbs and spices that would create that energy, and then prepare the meal focusing on those energies as you work with those herbs. It's impractical to name one recipe after a specific purpose. What will you do, make a cinnamon pie with cinnamon as the only ingredient? It makes no sense. So keep your intention in mind as you cook, and when it's time to add the ingredients whose energies you seek to use, say a quick prayer stating what you want it to help you with before adding it to your meal. So, let's get into some recipes you can try out!

Chicken Marbella

Thanks to Tasty.co for this recipe.

You'll Need:

- 3 lbs. chicken (protects your family and home)
- 1 head garlic, puréed or grated (offers protection)
- ¾ cup dried apricot (love)
- 3 tablespoons dried oregano (love, luck, protection)
- 2 teaspoons kosher salt (purifies and protects)
- ⅓ cup olive oil (fosters protection, peace, and loyalty)
- 3 red plums, pitted, quartered (encourages relaxation, love, and lust)
- 1 cup green olives (same as olive oil)
- ⅓ cup red wine vinegar (joy, health, physical strength)
- 6 cups couscous (nourishment, abundance)
- ⅓ cup dry rosé wine (joy, friendship)
- ½ cup brined capers (offers protection and love)
- ⅓ cup fresh basil, sliced thin (fosters prosperity and love)
- ⅔ cup light brown sugar (for improving mood, making people favor you, fostering love)
- 3 dried bay leaves (offers psychic protection)

Note that you can use a bubbly rosé wine instead of dry rosé wine. You can also use Himalayan pink salt instead of kosher salt.

Steps:

1. Use the salt to season the chicken evenly.

2. Rub 1 tablespoon of oregano and the garlic all over and into the chicken.

3. Using a glass baking dish about 9 x 13 inches, mix your olive oil, green olives, red wine vinegar, 2 tablespoons of oregano, capers, apricots, plums, and bay leaves.

4. Add the chicken to the dish and turn it in it to coat it with the mix. Let the skin side face upward.

5. With plastic wrap, cover the dish. Let the chicken sit in the fridge for 12 hours or overnight.

6. Preheat your oven to 375 degrees Fahrenheit.

7. Take the chicken out of the fridge. Give it half an hour to return to room temperature.

8. Pat the chicken dry with a paper towel.

9. Sprinkle the brown sugar onto the chicken skin.

10. Pour the rose around the chicken, but not onto the skin.

11. Bake for 35 to 40 minutes, or until your thermometer reads 160 degrees Fahrenheit when you insert it into the fold of a thigh close to the bone. The skin should be a nice, golden brown at this point.

12. Take the chicken out of the oven and let it cool for ten minutes. The temperature will go up by 5 degrees, thanks to the residual heat.

13. Serve the chicken with the sauce along with couscous. Use basil for garnishing.

Herbal Chicken Roast

You'll Need:

- 1 whole chicken (cleaned)
- 1 onion, cut into chunky bits (for getting rid of illness)
- ½ stick of salted butter (provides nourishment in any aspect of life)
- 1 handful of fresh herbs (combine lemon balm, thyme, and rosemary)
- 2 lemons, unpeeled, cut into chunks (for purification)
- Salt to taste (for protection and purification)
- Pepper to taste (also for protection and purification)

Steps:

1. Preheat your oven to 350 degrees Fahrenheit.
2. Clean your chicken if it's not already clean. Get rid of the innards, wash the whole thing with water, then pat it dry with paper towels to remove unnecessary moisture.
3. Squeeze one of the lemon chunks into the chicken's middle, then stuff the chicken with your onions, fresh herb, and the other lemon chunk. Use a string to tie the chicken's legs together, securing all the stuffing.
4. Put the chicken on a platter and let it bake for 20 minutes for every pound it weighs at 350 degrees Fahrenheit.
5. When there are only 40 minutes of baking left, or just before the skin gets crisp, melt your butter. Pour the melted butter over the chicken and slide it back into the oven.
6. Every ten to fifteen minutes, use the juices in the pan to baste the chicken.
7. Take it out and wait for it to cool before you serve.

What other recipes do you already know? Consider their spices, herbs, and other ingredients. How can you make them into magical spells? There are no limits, and there's no wrong way to do this.

Chapter Nine: Sacred Sabbats and Rituals

Hedge witches are in tune with nature, which means they are aware of its changes throughout the year. In this chapter, we will look at each of the eight festivals on the Wheel of the Year, focusing on the pagan aspects of the cycle.

Sabbats

Sabbats are holidays, and they are observed to mark the beginning of each season and their halfway points. They are spread out evenly all through the year. These Sabbats are rooted in Germanic and Celtic paganism. The word Sabbat is etymologically from the Hebrew language and is a central concept in Judaism. It's connected to the word "Sabbath," a time to gather to ensure certain rites and rituals are carried out.

The Eight Pagan Holidays or Sabbats

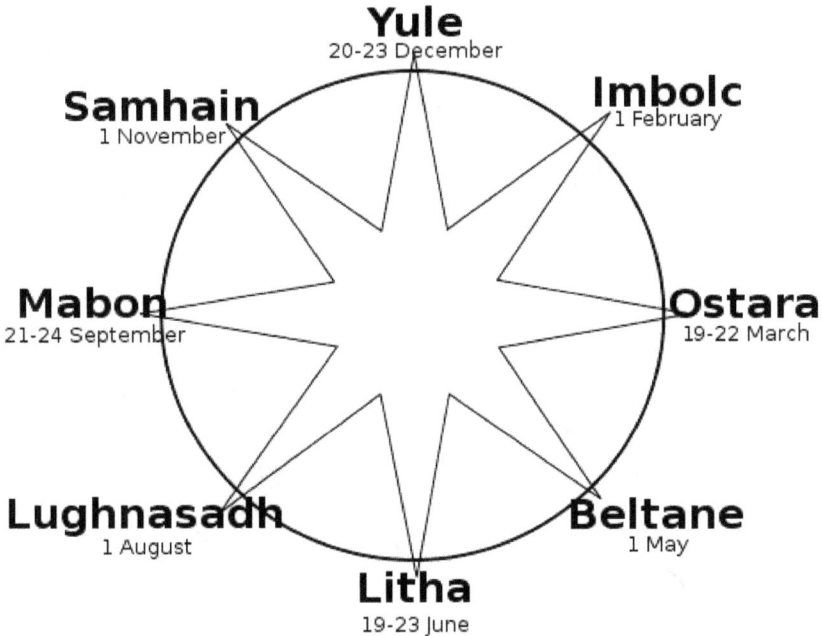

The eight pagan holidays calendar.
https://commons.wikimedia.org/wiki/File:Wheel_of_the_Year.svg

Yule: This is the Winter Solstice, which happens from December 20 to 23. At this point, you'll notice there are shorter days than usual. This is when everyone does what they must to be ready for the cold times to come. It's a good time to remember that the element of fire and the sun brings warmth to one and all, and they both make life possible on this planet. This is when people commonly decorate trees with food, specifically the kind of food that does well in cold times. This is meant to remind one and all that even when things get too dark and cold, growth is an ongoing process, and life will never end.

Christmas has certain traditions that it borrowed from this Sabbat. For instance, there's the yule log, originally intended to keep negative spirits from the Otherworld or around you and bless you with excellent luck. Then there's the mistletoe, which was used for the same purpose. Yule is a very old tradition, one of the oldest as far as human civilization is concerned. The winter solstice is marked on the year's shortest day.

How to Celebrate Yule

1. Yule is an excellent time to get together with your family and friends.

2. You could choose to light your Yule log, and you don't have to cut down a tree to do this.

3. Decorate your home with red and white.

4. Bring in the Yule energy with a gift for someone you love.

5. Wear a red ribbon as it symbolizes love and passion, but more importantly, it symbolizes love's eternal endurance through strife and trials.

6. Light candles and decorate with mistletoe, holly, ivy, yew, or pine boughs.

7. Hang baubles on the tree or around your home or spirit house to bring good luck in abundance all year round. You could also hang wind chimes which will quickly bring you into harmony with the moving energies of spirit as they sing their tune throughout your dwelling.

Imbolc: This falls on February 2 and is held in honor of the goddess Brigid, who blesses one and all with fertility. In other words, it's like a violent spring. This Sabbat is when you gather with others and celebrate the coming of spring, spring itself, and other good things in your life. It's also a time when we assess our personal lives to see if some improvement needs to be made to how we live our lives. It's when you set out candles, buns, and other foods and decorate them in honor of the coming of spring. It should remind one and all that the hard times are almost over.

Imbolc is also a sacred time to meditate on love which is meant to lead to happiness, peace, recognition from others around you, and a general sense of well-being. This reminds one and all that for something to truly be considered sacred, it must be about more than just your own life; it must also be about the well-being of others. For this reason, it was important in ancient times to do something that would benefit everyone living around you and yourself.

This is the midpoint between the winter solstice and spring equinox. During this time, you'll notice that the days are getting longer. That means it's time to enjoy lighter foods and, in general, more optimism in general. The fire element at work here is flame or light/heat, while water remains the element of purification. We do everything we can during this time to ensure a good growing season, so we can grow our food and create wealth for ourselves and our families. The best way to do that is to ensure the past year's leftover and bad energy or spirits don't stick around but rather move on. We do that by sweeping our homes and businesses clean using reed brooms. The old furniture is removed, and new, fresh furniture is brought in. We also have the tradition of lighting a candle on the windowsill during this time to signal that spring has arrived and life will continue onward. This holiday isn't entirely about fertility as many people think. It's about celebrating the abundance it brings in general.

How to Celebrate Imbolc

1. You could make a feast in honor of Brigid and all the blessings she has brought to your life and to all those around you. Have a good time and eat, drink, and be merry!

2. Light a candle on the windowsill to signal new growth and the future ahead of you.

3. Celebrate the arrival of spring by decorating with flowers, plants, wheat sheaves, or new growth in general. For example, if it's February 2, you could decorate fresh-cut spruce branches sprinkled with winter salt (see description below). This is meant to signify renewal and a clean slate for you after the harsh winter months.

4. You could also decorate the house with flowers or wheat stalks.

5. Make wheat saffron buns, which will remind you of the importance of food in your life and represent an ancient form of this holiday.

6. Make sure your home is clean, as well as your spirit house or temple if you have one in your home. Then you'll know that the bad spirits that may have been lingering around since the past year are now gone and won't be coming back anytime soon. And if they do, at

least you'll know it was because they were invited.

7. Create a wish and make it known to the goddess, then get back to living the rest of your life knowing that Brigid has taken your wish into account, but it is up to you to make the most of whatever happens.

Ostara: This is the Spring Equinox, and it falls between March 19 and 22. That means that at this time it's sunny and warm. It's also a day for renewal and renewal of the natural state of things. This is when you do what is necessary to ensure your life goes well, both personally and professionally. We're talking about ensuring there's nothing negative in your life that needs to be removed, as well as making sure everything you added over the winter has a chance to bloom. This is also a time for romantic love, fidelity in marriage, one-on-one friendship relationships, membership in a group or society, and work partnerships. You'll notice you're more interested in sex and romance than in religion, which is also a sign of spring.

The elements of water and spirit merge at this time, which means it is time to make peace with existing conditions and with the past. You'll invite others up to your home for food and conversation, which is meant to give each other strength. Because it's the Spring Equinox, this is also the best time of year to plant new seeds or plants if you can add some beauty to your home. It's also when we move from our homes into our new homes and into acquiring new careers. The Christian holiday Easter borrows heavily from this feast and is actually in honor of the goddess Eostre, who is of Germanic origin.

How to Celebrate Ostara

1. You could decorate with flowers and plants, especially seeds and saplings, if you have them.

2. You could also create traditional Easter baskets filled with foods such as eggs, bread, and wine.

3. You can also decorate to celebrate love, oaths of fidelity, loyalty, and friendship by bringing in a bouquet of flowers for your porch or front door or by putting up a new broom in your home if you haven't had one for many months.

4. You can also wait until April 1 to work on all future vows of fidelity, friendship, and romantic love during Ostara.

5. You can make sure you decorate your home with flowers, plants, wheat sheaves, or even indoor plants to signify the renewal of life.

6. Try to find a new job, whether that's in your current career or an entirely different one, to ensure you're getting ahead in life and allow the flow of Ostara's fertile energy. Make sure you live up to your vows of fidelity.

7. Take walks in the woods and nature to help cleanse your spirit and make peace with the past and the current natural world around you.

Beltane: This is celebrated on Mayday, which is May 1. It's also called the Festival of Fire and marks the time between the spring equinox and the coming summer solstice. At this point, spring has made progress, and it's starting to give way to more warmth and longer days that mark summer. The etymological root of Beltane is from Bel, a Celtic god, and *teine,* a Gaelic word that translates to "fire." At this time, you're expected to show your appreciation for spring, thankful that it makes all things fertile physically and in other aspects of your life. At this time, people dance around the maypole, often with crowns of flowers on their heads. It's also believed that the veil between the physical world and the Otherworld is thin at this time, and therefore it's a good idea to perform magic that requires extra power. It's also a time to celebrate the coming harvest.

How to Celebrate Beltane

1. You could also decorate your home to honor the coming summer using plants such as wheat sheaves, wheat stalks, corn stalks, and even fresh-picked holly twigs.

2. Honor the god Bel by offering him grains on your altar.

3. Celebrate the coming harvest by placing three glasses of beer or ale in a triangle shape around your home for the following three days.

4. Celebrate the birth of love, friendship, and devotion to your favorite deity or goddess at this time.

5. Make sure you dance around the maypole with your friends and have lots of joy, laughter, and fun.

6. You can also clean your home by removing unnecessary things.

7. You can plant seeds and saplings to honor fertility and new growth, as well as to honor life.

Litha: This is marked between June 19 and 23. It's also known as the summer solstice or midsummer, and unlike Yule, it is the day of the year with the longest day and the shortest night. You can do the work you must at this time, but you should also celebrate as you now have long days that will allow enough time to achieve goals and be merry. This is when many will get engaged, and it's also when blessings are pronounced over the land, so the harvest will be bountiful indeed. Traditionally, this time is celebrated with torchlight processions through the land and bonfires. These are meant to remind one and all of the power and glory of the sun, which will eventually lose its power over time as summer gives way to winter once more.

How to Celebrate Litha

1. You can decorate your home with plants and flowers such as roses, honeysuckle, and foxglove.

2. This is a time to catch up on any summer goals.

3. You can honor the deities of fertility and the sun with your home decoration or by placing their statues or pictures around the place.

4. You can celebrate the coming of love, friendship, and romance with those you love.

5. Make offerings to the deities by throwing food onto bonfires, although not just any food, but fruit and nuts such as chestnuts and walnuts, as well as milk or milk products such as butter and cream, to honor these gods.

6. Take lots of walks outside to enjoy the summer air and to help cleanse your mind of everything you've been thinking about for so long.

7. Plant new seeds and saplings to honor fertility and prosperity.

Lughnasadh: This is also called the first harvest, and it's marked on August 1. It's a time between summer and autumn when the very first harvests are brought in from the fields. It's about celebrating that the earth worked with the sun to yield more than enough fruit and grain for one and all. It's important to give thanks for the good that we receive. This is such a joyful time that many also choose this holiday to get married. The Sabbat is named after Lugh, the light god. It is said that Tailtiu, his mother, helped to prepare Ireland's lands so that crops could be planted successfully.

How to Celebrate Lughnasadh

1. You can decorate your home with plants such as wheat sheaves, wheat stalks, corn stalks, and even fresh-picked holly twigs.

2. You can also decorate your home with pumpkins and painted eggs to celebrate the year's first harvests.

3. At this time, many will make large bonfires where food is traditionally cooked in large cauldrons to allow the flames to impart good luck and blessings of prosperity to the land. This is because Lughnasadh is a time when fire is believed to be very powerful and magical.

4. Make offerings to the sun god and goddess by throwing food onto bonfires.

5. Celebrate your mother or father that evening with a feast, especially since you're celebrating their harvest.

6. You can also pray for power over the year and abundance in all you do by holding a ritual around the fire to help balance the energies of your home to help you all be prosperous throughout all aspects of life (work, love, and play).

7. Wear new clothes that signify fertility and abundance at this time, if possible, as well as new shoes if footwear is necessary to do what must be done during this time.

Mabon: This is also known as the autumn equinox, which holds from September 21 to 24. It's when autumn comes, marking the time for the harvest to be reaped. It's a time of plenty, and all the labor that people have put into their projects comes to fruition at this time so that preparations can be made for the cold months to come.

How to Celebrate Mabon

1. You can decorate your altar with fresh fruit such as apples and pears.

2. You can also hang dried fruit such as raisins and cranberries around your home to signify the abundance of good fruit harvested at harvest time.

3. You can make paper mâché masks that look like pumpkins and scarecrows made out of straw to honor the coming of fall and its harvesting seasons.

4. Try to help friends and family who are struggling during this time by giving them support and prayers.

5. You can celebrate the coming of love, friendship, and prosperity by giving thanks to your favorite deity at this time as well.

6. Clean your home by getting rid of unnecessary things.

7. Wear jewelry made of silver or moonstones, which are believed to celebrate the god of the earth at this time, and give thanks for what you have received.

Samhain: This is also known as Halloween and is celebrated either on October 31 or November 1. It's a magical time of the year, being the only other time the veil between our world and the Otherworld is thin, letting the living and dead interact and draw on each other's power as needed. It's also called All Hallow's Eve, the time for one and all to pay their respects to familiars, family, and other loved ones who have passed. To celebrate this time, it is customary to have Jack Lanterns made from pumpkins to light a pathway for those who have passed on, so they can find their way to their next adventure. You can use this time to seek guidance, get rid of stubbornly lingering negativity, seek help with difficult or confusing situations, and begin the new year on the right footing for a higher chance you'll end it successfully.

How to Celebrate Samhain

1. You can decorate your home with fresh fruit as well as pumpkins, candles, and Jack O'Lanterns.

2. You can also make a special meal, such as a feast, around the table where you and your loved ones are seated.

3. Set intentions for the New Year, saying what you will do and want to achieve.

4. Bury and burn old things that have no meaning or power to allow for new things to affect your life. This includes burning candles as offerings as well.

5. Make sure you use this Sabbat's energy to eliminate any bad habits.

6. You can also reset the energies of your home by burning sage or ridding yourself of clutter and unwanted items that may take up space inside your home.

7. Wear dark colors at this time so that you can make contact with the dead and seek guidance on how to accomplish what you wish to do in your life.

Chapter Ten: Your Hedge Spell Book

People often wonder when the best time is to practice spells. It doesn't matter if you do it in the morning, noon, or at night. You could have "set times" and still not get results because you're not in the right frame of mind or your intentions aren't clear. In other words, the only thing that matters with a spell is you know exactly what you want it to accomplish, and you're in a state of mind that is completely focused, free from distractions and worries.

To borrow from the psychedelic community, you could say effective spells are less about time and more about "set and setting," with the *set* being your frame of mind before, during, and after the spell, and the *setting* being your location. You should perform the spell somewhere you won't be disturbed. Make it somewhere that feels right to you, so you can focus on the task at hand and not lose energy trying to make an unfamiliar or uncomfortable space comfortable.

A final note: While specific herbs are mentioned in each spell, please note there's no rule that says you must work with them. For instance, if an abundance spell calls for High John the Conqueror, but you don't have that on hand, feel free to replace that with another spice or herbs like mint or bay leaf.

Magic Money Spell

This spell involves creating a money bag that will draw prosperity to you or whoever you perform it for. Please be certain that you're ready for the money to come and will be responsible with it, because it works like, well, like a charm.

You'll Need:

- Allspice (1 pinch)
- Some drops of bergamot essential oil
- A black marker
- A paper bag
- Play money of different denominations

Steps:

1. Use your marker to draw any currency signs you want on it. Make sure they're prominent. More is better.
2. Put the play money into the bag.
3. Add in your allspice and bergamot oil.
4. Squeeze the top of the bag closed and give the bag a shake. You want the herbs to be all over every bill in the bag. As you shake it, affirm that money comes to you quickly and easily.
5. When you've finished, move around your space, putting the paper bills in different spots where no one will move them.
6. When you've finished, carefully fold the paper baggie, and keep it somewhere safe. Expect that money will begin flowing to you from unexpected sources.

Wallet Charging Spell

If you feel like money hasn't really been flowing lately, it could be because the energy of abundance and flow is being blocked by your inability or refusal to be on the lookout for it. Fortunately, there's a way to get things flowing again, and the wallet charging spell is a very potent one that will bring you as much financial relief as you require.

You'll Need:

- A pen
- A blank check (you can use an actual check or print one off the internet)
- Your wallet or purse
- 1 teaspoon of dill

Steps:

1. First, figure out how much money you need to get by each month and still have enough to spare.
2. Next, fill in the check to yourself with that amount.
3. Fold the check-in half and put the dill in the crease.
4. Fold the check with the dill as tight as possible to seal in the herb.
5. Put this folded check in your wallet. It will draw money to you

Plentiful Pockets Charm

People don't understand about being abundant and prosperous because money and wealth can come from sources other than the usual or expected. Being open-minded to the flow of abundance like this puts you in a position to receive more of the universe's bounty. The plentiful pockets charm is a good one to help you open your eyes to the opportunities to make wealth that are all around you.

You'll Need:

- A string or some twine
- A square piece of green flannel (at least 4 inches on each side)
- 1 Piece of High John the Conqueror root (draws abundance)
- 1 Teaspoon chamomile (dried)

Steps:

1. Set the flannel on your altar.
2. On the flannel, place the High John the Conqueror root and the chamomile.
3. Use the flannel to create a pouch of sorts by pulling the corners together. As you do this, say, or concentrate on your intention to receive money and wealth that blesses one and all.
4. Use the twine or string to tie the pouch securely. Take this around with you to use it to attract money-making opportunities and financial blessings that are nothing short of amazing to you.

Blossoming Money

This spell calls for apples, which represent the energy of harvest, prosperity, and bounty. You can do this spell whenever you want, but if you perform this when the moon waxes, you will have an explosive inflow of money or money-making opportunities.

You'll Need:

- Apple blossoms (dried)
- New pennies
- A lidded glass jar

Steps:

1. Put all the apple blossoms and pennies you can into the jar. Make sure you mix them up instead of putting them in layers.

2. Cover the jar and hold it in both hands as you set an intention or say a prayer that your finances will continue to prosper.

3. Take this jar to your yard and find a nice spot where it can't be unearthed to bury.

4. Got an apple tree? You can bury your jar beneath that instead of any random spot to take advantage of the tree's energy to boost your spell.

Love by Candlelight Spell

If you're ready for love after having been on your own for far too long, this is a wonderful spell to use to get you open to the possibility of receiving love and drawing your perfect match your way.

You'll Need:

- 1 pink candle
- Dried, powdered dill
- Almond or grape seed or jojoba oil

Steps:

1. Use a sharp object to carve a heart into the side of the candle or carve the word, Love. If you want, you can do both and add other symbols representing the idea of being loved. As you carve, chant, or sing the word "love," let it fill your heart.

2. When you've finished carving, rub some oil on your candle.

3. Take your candle and dress it with the dill. Let it be completely dressed.

4. Light your candle and set it down. Bring your gaze to the flame and feel its energy entering and enveloping you inside.

5. Now, imagine that you are full of loving energy. You can imagine it as a beautiful, soft pink light. See and feel it as it radiates outside you, filling the whole room and then the whole world. Realize that you deserve to love and be loved as you want. Affirm that you're worthy of love in its fullest, truest form.

6. Now, imagine being embraced by a lover. Feel what it's like to have their skin on yours. Allow yourself to smile and notice the warmth in your chest.

7. Let the candle burn until it goes out on its own, and then bury it outside close to your home.

Heart "Unbreaker" Spell

It's not easy to deal with breakups and betrayals in love. It's often hard to mend what's broken. With this spell, though, you will be able to heal much faster and better than you ever thought possible while integrating the lessons you learned from your relationship. As this is a spell meant to rid yourself of something, you can take advantage of the waning moon phase. However, if you can't wait till then, feel free to do it when you need to.

You'll Need:

- A bonfire or a fireplace

- Flammable items connected to whoever broke your heart

- Witch hazel branches (dried)

- Stinging nettle branches (dried)

- 1 Pinch of ginger (dried, powdered)

- A paper bag

Steps:

1. Take all the things that belong to your ex-lover and put them into the bag.
2. Put the witch hazel and stinging nettle into the bag.
3. Fold the top of the bag shut, and then fold the bag itself as small as you can, so it's not bigger than a packet.
4. Get your fire ready. When it's blazing hot, put the packet into the flame, aiming so that it lands right in the middle. Then, as it burns, repeat, "I intend to release this person." Intend that they no longer have power over you and that all the bonds keeping you together are hereby dissolved for eternity; if you feel the need to cry, allow the tears to flow and draw on their energy to empower your spell.
5. Toss the dried ginger in, intending that it boosts the speed at which your heart recovers.
6. When the packet and its contents are completely burned, let the fire die out naturally, and wait for everything to cool down.

7. Take the cool ashes out and take them as far from your home or ritual space as possible. Throw them out somewhere with a lot of wind to carry them away so that you no longer feel bad about things ending.

Love in the Pocket Charm

High John the Conqueror root is also very useful for fertility and sexual magnetism. You'll find that working with it allows you to be very confident in your sexuality, attracting love and suitable partners.

You'll Need:

- Red thread
- High John the Conqueror root
- 1 Red candle

Steps:

1. Carve the word "love" and the shape of a heart into the side of your red candle.
2. Light the candle.
3. While it burns, hold the High John the Conqueror root in both hands, and in your mind's eye, imagine your hands imbuing it with the power of love and raw attraction.
4. Take the red thread and tie it around the root, intending that lovers will be drawn to you.
5. Keep this in your pocket and watch the magic happen.

Pocket Protection Charm

It's a good idea to always have something to keep you safe no matter where you go, and so there's no better charm than one designed to do just that and can fit into your pocket.

You'll Need:

- Red yarn or string
- A square of red fabric (3 inches on all sides)
- Amethyst (just one small piece)
- ½ Teaspoon rosemary (dried)
- ½ Teaspoon peppermint (dried)

Steps:

1. Set your red fabric on your altar.
2. Put the herbs and the crystal in the middle of the fabric.
3. Hold the fabric by the corners and pull it up to form a little pouch.
4. Use the red yarn to secure the fabric into a pouch. As you do so, intend to always be safe and always protected.
5. You can wear this around your neck or carry it in your pocket wherever you go.

Basil Protection Bag

Basil is amazing for staying safe from bad energy, deliberate magical attacks, curses, and bad luck. All you need to do is use it in your bath each day.

You'll Need:

- Fresh basil (you can use dry basil if that's not available)
- A cheesecloth bag with a drawstring

Steps:

1. Fill the bag with fresh basil
2. Run a bath. Make it a warm one. Let the bag hang from the faucet to let the water run through it.
3. Take a bath as usual.
4. When you're ready to come out, intend that all things negative have left your body, mind, and spirit, then come out.
5. Take the bag outside your home and bury it far away.

Mugwort Deep Sleep Spell

This is a good spell for when you're stressed out by the events of the day and you would like to sleep but are having trouble because you're anxious.

You'll Need:

- 1 teaspoon honey
- 1 cup of hot water
- 1 mug
- 1 teaspoon mugwort (dried)

Steps:

1. Put the mugwort into your mug.
2. Pour in hot water and let the mugwort steep for 15 minutes.
3. With a strainer, separate the tea from the plant matter.
4. Add honey if you want.
5. Before drinking it, make up your mind that you'll have a good night's sleep and pleasant dreams too. Then drink your tea.

Mugwort tea is not recommended for those who are nursing or pregnant.

Menstrual Pain Relief Spell

For some women, menstrual cycles can be incredibly frustrating. They have to deal with mood switches, irritability, anxiety, loads of pain, restlessness, and so on. This is an excellent spell if you know that your periods tend to be very problematic. You can work to make sure that you feel better.

You'll Need:

- 1 tablespoon rue
- Garnet
- Carnelian
- Moonstone
- 1 White candle
- 1 Red drawstring bag (small)

Steps:

1. Light your candle.
2. Spend five minutes looking into the flame.
3. As you look into the flame, imagine that your body is healing in your mind's eye. Imagine that a white light moves through your body, removing all the pain and making you feel more comfortable as it leaves with the bleeding.
4. Put the rue into the drawstring pouch while you say a little prayer or affirmation, intending that you will not be defeated or made to feel low by your cycle. Affirm that you are powerful, strong, and healthy and that all discomfort leaves your body now.
5. Close the bag by pulling the drawstring as you affirm that you take back your power and strength from the pain you feel.
6. Take this pouch with you every time it's that time of the month so you can feel better physically and bring balance to your emotions.

Third Eye Opening Spell

You need your third eye to help you to ride the hedge. The more open it is, the easier this experience will be for you, and the more profound your insights will be.

You'll Need:

- 1 drawstring bag (a small one)
- Some mugwort sprigs (make them fresh)
- Some chips of sandalwood

Steps:

1. Mix the sandalwood and mugwort, then use them to fill the drawstring pouch.

2. Lie comfortably, shut your eyes, and let the bag sit in the middle of your forehead, between your brows, and above eye level.

3. Take some calming deep breaths and let yourself release all thoughts and concerns.

4. In your mind's eye, see yourself become more spiritually awakened, enlightened, and open to communication with your divine self. See radiant white light as it flows from the universe, moving through the herbs in your pouch, going straight into your third eye, causing it to open even more.

5. Allow yourself to soak in the power of this radiant white light as you affirm that you have more wisdom and are in touch with your intuition. Affirm that your third eye is wide open and healthy.

Psychic Booster Amulet

If you want to be more in touch with your spirit guides and be able to hear when they have critical messages for you, then this is an amulet worth making and keeping on your person. As you continue to wear it, it will make it easier for you to access visions, gain wisdom, and receive insight from your ancestors and other guides you have.

You'll Need:

- 1 Teaspoon sage (dried)
- 1 Teaspoon cinnamon (ground)
- 1 Leather cord (at least 18 inches in length)
- Modeling clay

Steps

1. Roll a bit of modeling clay in your hands until it's soft and easy to manipulate.

2. Add sage and cinnamon, working them into the clay with your fingers while imagining you're opening up your heart and soul to receiving messages from the spirit. You can work the clay into a little circle or any other shape you like that is magically significant to you.

3. Let the clay dry, and then attach it to your cord or chain. This will make it easier for you to receive spiritual messages clearly.

4. Whenever you want to receive guidance about a specific message, you can hold this in your dominant hand as you say a prayer or set an intention to receive insight on whatever topic is bothering you.

5. If you like, you can place this beneath your pillow at night while going to sleep, thinking about what you need guidance on. You will have dreams where your guide will communicate the answers you seek. It is important that you sleep with the mindset that you will definitely receive answers.

Conclusion

For many years, the author of this book practiced hedge witchcraft and, during the course of doing so, learned a great deal about trees, herbs, and plants and their nature. It was also possible to learn how they interact with the environment, which was not only an intriguing study but also a vital tool to aid her family and her community.

You may learn, as she did, some important life lessons from practicing hedge witchcraft. The first lesson is that learning anything new is never too late. You can reach a deep understanding of certain topics by learning, such as reading books, watching videos, attending classes, etc. There is no shortage of sources for learning your craft if you should choose to go down this path.

The second lesson is to think outside the box. There are so many tools and ways to learn that it can be helpful to pose questions within your family or circle of friends regarding what you have just learned. For example, what could you do with this newly acquired information? By asking these questions, you can grow and expand on your beliefs, or you'll see if someone else has already done something similar, which may lead to further learning or borrowing from their craft or practices.

Whatever you do, do not neglect the power of hedge riding. Use it to your advantage to communicate with guides and get higher knowledge about the secrets locked within certain herbs and plants and how you can best use them. There are more things to learn about these gifts of nature than any book on the planet could possibly teach you. Some plants may respond to you differently than how they would to another witch. So, use your hedge riding sessions to learn more about your craft from the wiser spirits.

Hedge witchcraft is a practice that teaches you to honor and respect the natural world (especially trees and plants) and people. It teaches you to be a part of the ecosystem and love what comes from the trees instead of simply taking from it. If you are ever in doubt, ask the plants or trees for permission to use what you need. There are many ways to conduct this sort of hedge witchcraft, and you can talk to the trees or plants, sing to them, whisper to them, or use a pendulum, divining rod, or rune staves.

Any method that allows you to communicate with the tree is acceptable. Simply put, it is a very personal practice – something that must be done on an individual level and not simply copied from someone else. So, if the herbs or your intuition tell you that you can use them for a certain intention, then feel free to do that. Make every spell and ritual your own because the power lies in your uniqueness.

Finally, you need to remember that this is a practice. In other words, reading is only one step. You have to actually craft spells and get in touch with your deity to see results. You can't read about one thing and decide you've mastered it. Put everything you learn here to the test, and if you don't succeed at first, that doesn't mean it doesn't work. Get clear in your intentions and try again; *never forget to record what you are doing in your grimoire.*

Here's another book by Mari Silva that you might like

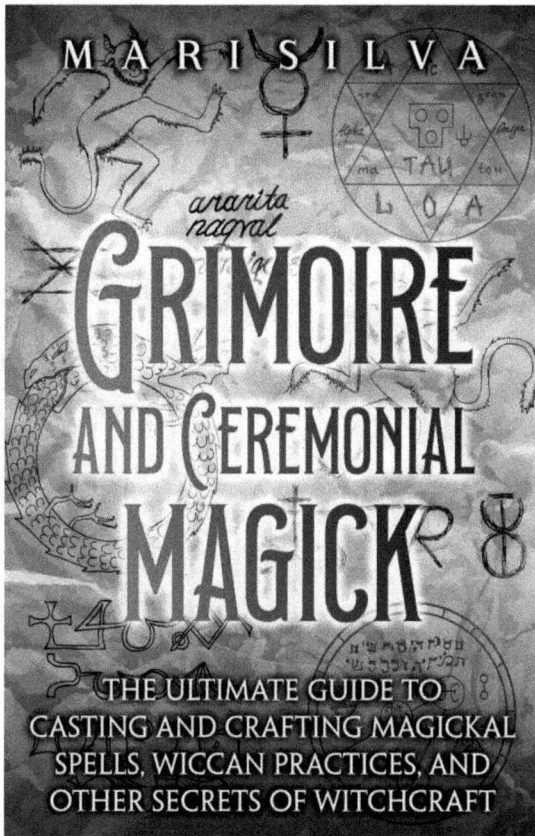

Your Free Gift
(only available for a limited time)

Thanks for getting this book! If you want to learn more about various spirituality topics, then join Mari Silva's community and get a free guided meditation MP3 for awakening your third eye. This guided meditation mp3 is designed to open and strengthen ones third eye so you can experience a higher state of consciousness. Simply visit the link below the image to get started.

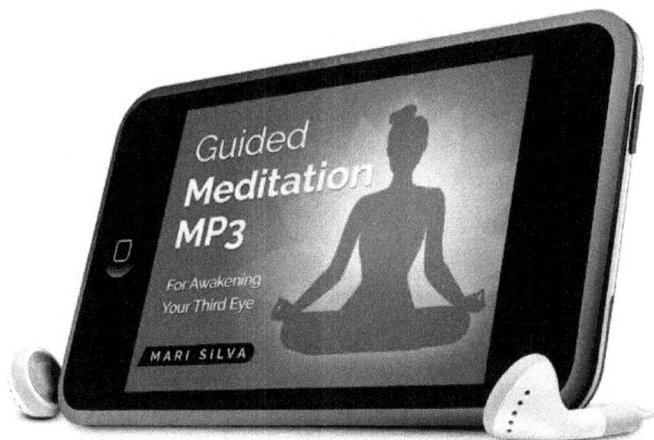

https://spiritualityspot.com/meditation

References

Beth, R. (2018). The Green Hedge Witch. The Cordwood Press.

Beth, R. (2018). The Hedge Witch's Way: Magical Spirituality for the Lone Spell caster. The Cordwood Press.

Beth, R. (2018). Spell craft for Hedge Witches: A Guide to Healing Our Lives. The Cordwood Press.

De Varies, E. (2008). Hedge-Rider: Witches and the Underworld. Padraig Publishing.

Dugan, E. (2012). Garden Witch's Herbal: Green Magic, Herbalism & Spirituality. Llewellyn Worldwide.

Greenfield, T. (2014). Witchcraft Today-60 Years On. John Hunt Publishing.

Griffith, D. B. (2009). Lithe 2005. Lulu. Com.

Kane, A. (2021). Herbal Magic: A Handbook of Natural Spells, Charms, and Potions. Wellfleet Press.

Moura, A. (2014). Green Witchcraft: Folk Magic, Fairy Lore & Herb Craft. Llewellyn Worldwide.

Moura, A. (2020). Green Witchcraft IV: Walking the Faerie Path. Llewellyn Worldwide.

Moura, A. (2003). Grimoire for the Green Witch: A Complete Book of Shadows (Vol. 5). Llewellyn Worldwide.

Murphy-Hiscock, A. (2006). The Way Of The Green Witch: Rituals, Spells, And Practices to Bring You Back to Nature. Simon and Schuster.

Murphy-Hiscock, A. (2017). The green witch: your complete guide to the natural magic of herbs, flowers, essential oils, and more. Simon and Schuster

www.ingramcontent.com/pod-product-compliance
Lightning Source LLC
Chambersburg PA
CBHW071904090426
42811CB00004B/733